1 Colorado History Museum
  Byers-Evans House Museum
  Grant-Humphreys Mansion

2. El Pueblo History Museum

3. Fort Garland Museum

4. Pike's Stockade

5. Fort Vasquez Museum

6. Georgetown Loop Historic Mining & Railroad Park

7. Healy House Museum & Dexter Cabin

8. Trinidad History Museum

9. Ute Indian Museum

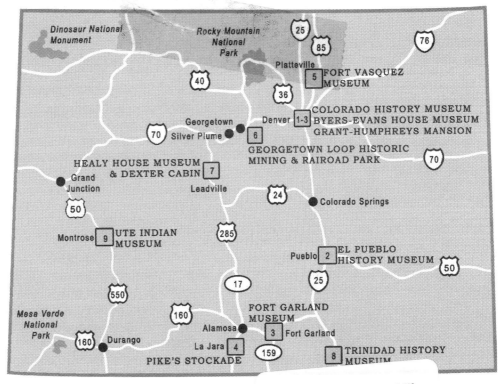

D1416005

Colorado

Published by
Volunteers of the

COLORADO
HISTORICAL SOCIETY

1300 Broadway
Denver, Colorado 80203

© 2005 Volunteers of the
Colorado Historical
Society

More Across Colorado

ISBN 0-9770423-0-8
$21.95

COVER ILLUSTRATION

Acrylic painting by Colorado artist Patti Russell

COOKBOOK COMMITTEE

Betty Heid	Chair & Project Manager
Ed Ellis	Historical Photos & Text Researcher
Margaret Greivel	Research assistant
Steve Longsdorf	Research assistant
Sally Longwell	Recipe Solicitation & Testing Team Leader
Gloria Rosener	President, Colorado Historical Society Volunteers
John Russell	Design and Production Director
Paulette Whitcomb	Editor

CONTENTS

More Across Colorado

FOREWORD
Tom "Dr. Colorado" Noel

Volunteers have long done the digging in Colorado. In the beginning, volunteers dug to find gold and to plant crops. The first cooks, politicians, ladies of the night, journalists, police, fire lads, teachers, clergymen and nearly everyone else volunteered. Creating Colorado was a labor of love.

Another labor of love is this gold mine of recipes and recollections crafted by countless volunteers who have donated their time, talent and treasures to furthering the work of the Colorado Historical Society by bringing pleasure and information to the public.

In 1962, the Society's Volunteers published **Pioneer Potluck**, a cookbook of historical recipes. **Across Colorado** in 1997 was a bigger, better, and more ambitious effort focused on contemporary recipes. After four editions, it is out of print. A yelp of delight is occasionally heard from those fortunate few who find a copy to purchase. **More Across Colorado** is a compelling mix of the old and new. The traditional fare is definitely here, but sometimes it wears fresh herbs in its hair. Then again, many recipes are as fresh as a High Plains sunrise, with nutritional awareness and today's international flavors: Greek Orzo Salad, Jalapeño White Sauce, Penne alla Zucca, Romaine Chiffonade with Pesto Vinaigrette …

Many of these recipes are over a century old: From Germany, old-fashioned butter cookies and sour cream cookies; pancakes from Sweden; a Norwegian custard. The apple pudding and rice dish that helped pay off a church debt exemplify the Colorado tradition of volunteers feeding the community for a good cause. Try a 110-year-old, unretouched formula for Italian Bananas from Trinidad. Who knows how old are Ireland's Colcannon and Yugoslavia's Djuvec? A High Country twist updates Tuscany's Tozzetti, however. And Polenta is microwaved, a change from the days when the contributor's "Italian grandfather stirred for hours with a wooden paddle."

More Across Colorado

In your hands is the best Colorado butter caramel recipe ever. Mrs. Russell Stover lusted after this original recipe and offered a huge sum to its creator. Mrs. Stover never got her hands on it, but it is here for you. This sweet book (just reading the recipe names makes one swoon) is rich in desserts, candies and confections – none of which have any calories at Colorado's exalted elevations. And you will probably need something sweet after entrées like the Genuine Green Chile. (The cook tells me she got the recipe from a priest – but not in the confessional.)

Epicurean havens in our mountain towns contributed hearty concoctions. Colorado's First Lady Frances Owens donated two recipes. Colorado's exalted food historian, Sam Arnold, at The Fort Restaurant, a genuine re-creation in the Denver foothills of Bent's Old Fort, shares his formula for Teriyaki Quail. Says Sam'l, "Recipes are a lot like road maps. Where you start, how you travel, and how you end up are strictly up to you."

Every recipe herein was tested at least three times, by three different volunteers, who improved on any recipe that could be perfected. Each time they tested the product on best friends and kin. All of these folks are alive and prospering.

You cannot go wrong with this bonanza of a book. Compiled from contributions from every corner of our colorful state, **More Across Colorado** offers you an unusual combination. This book offers a cookbook; personal recollections; and photographs, many heretofore unpublished, mostly from the Colorado Historical Society's superb collection of more than 700,000 images. As a special extra, this work offers an after-dinner delight – historical vignettes from the Society's fabulous Historic Marker Program, once known as Roadside Markers.

Bon appétit and happy trails.

More Across Colorado

INTRODUCTION   *Betty Heid, Committee Chair and Project Manager*

From Appetizers to Desserts, from Entrées to Miscellaneous, this cookbook will take you on a fascinating history tour throughout Colorado. Many hundreds of hours went into the selection of the recipes and photos and historical text. The editing and compiling of the book were daunting tasks very well done. We hope you will enjoy your travel through Colorado history as you prepare the many interesting and flavorful recipes within the pages of this cookbook.

These recipes were contributed by cooks from our major cities – Denver, Colorado Springs, Pueblo – as well as from our rural areas – Trinidad, Fraser, Windsor, to name just a few. This collection of recipes captures the essence and spirit of Colorado cooking. All recipes were tested numerous times to ensure that cooks with a wide range of skill levels would enjoy preparing them. They were also tested for high altitude and ease of preparation. The testers devoted countless hours preparing these recipes and serving them to family and friends to assure that only the best were included for your pleasure.

Many of these recipes have been handed down from generation to generation and are shared here publicly for the first time; they are the culinary legacy of multi-generations of Colorado families. We hope these collected recipes will become favorites with you and your families for many years to come.

This book is dedicated to the numerous volunteers that made it possible: the recipe contributors, the testers, and especially the cookbook committee. Special thanks go to Patti Russell, a very talented local artist, for the original cover design.

All proceeds benefit the Volunteers of the Colorado Historical Society. The volunteer organization supports activities at the Colorado Historical Society Museum and the other CHS regional museums and properties throughout the state.

More Across Colorado

SPECIAL DAYS AND SPECIAL FOODS
Georgianna Contiguglia,
President, Colorado Historical Society

Special foods

and their rituals

are inextricable

parts of our families

and our holidays –

and thus of the

history of our lives.

No matter what your ethnic or religious backgrounds, special foods are inextricably associated with special family events and holiday celebrations.

My husband, Bob, comes from a large Italian-American family, and all the women – and some of the men – are good cooks. Bob tells me that his Nonna (his Italian Grandmother) used to cook for days before holiday get-togethers. The meals she prepared would include the Italian part – an antipasto, salad, soup and pasta – and then the American part – turkey, stuffing, mashed potatoes and such. He tells me that he was thirteen years old before he was able to get beyond the pasta course!

In my family, there were special foods and food-preparation activities that appeared in an annual cycle. Making Christmas cookies was a favorite of mine when I was a youngster. My little sister and I would take most of a Saturday baking up batches of sugar cookies that we painstakingly cut into intricate holiday shapes, such as stars, angels, Santas

More Across Colorado

and so on. Then we would decorate these delicacies with homemade frosting in many colors, swirled and spritzed over the cookies and sprinkled with colored sugars. The ritual told us that Christmas was near, and we knew that Santa would enjoy his late-night snack of cookies and milk that we left for him on Christmas Eve.

There was another very special ritual that we followed whenever it snowed enough for school to be called off. My Dad was a teacher, so a snow day was a holiday for him as well as for the kids. He was always the first to awake in the morning, and when he learned that a snow day had been called, he would trudge out in the blizzard to our local bakery, where the morning bread was rising. He would purchase some of the raw bread dough and bring it home, where he would then fry up *malasada*. The Portuguese equivalent of Indian fry bread, this recipe had been a part of his Portuguese family's cooking tradition. We would awaken to the wonderful smells of bacon and *malasada*, which we would devour before heading out to build our snowmen and snow forts. A delicious dish is worth passing along to another generation, so I have made a tradition of making this breakfast dish for my own family when we've been up in the mountains on ski trips.

I know you will enjoy the many scrumptious recipes, those bits of personal history, handed along to you in this beautiful cookbook.

More Across Colorado

COLORADO
HISTORICAL
SOCIETY

1300 Broadway
Denver, Colorado 80203

Caprese Salad Bites

60 red and/or yellow cherry tomatoes
1 pound fresh mozzarella, cut into small cubes
¼ cup olive oil
3 tablespoons balsamic vinegar
fresh chopped basil for garnish

Serves: 20

With a serrated knife, cut off top of each tomato. Remove seeds with a melon baller. Cut a thin slice off bottom of each tomato. Place upside down on paper towels to drain. Stand upright on serving dish. Place a mozzarella cube in each tomato. Drizzle with olive oil and vinegar. Garnish with basil.

Cheese Salmon Spread

1 cup crushed Club Crackers (about 24)
3 tablespoons butter, melted
2 8-ounce packages cream cheese, softened
3 eggs
¼ cup sour cream
1 pound canned salmon, cleaned, drained
        and flaked
juice from ½ lemon
2 tablespoons grated onion
⅛ teaspoon freshly ground pepper
Topping:
½ cup sour cream
¼ cup mayonnaise
fresh dill for garnish, *or* dried dill weed

Cooking time: 1 hour
Serves: 10 to 15

Thoroughly mix cracker crumbs and melted butter. Press into bottom of 9-inch spring form pan. Bake at 350° for 10 minutes. Remove from oven and cool. Beat together cream cheese, eggs and sour cream. Add salmon, lemon juice, onion and pepper, and continue to beat to mix well. Pour over cooled crust.
Bake at 325° for 50 to 55 minutes, or until middle is set.
Remove from oven and run sharp knife around pan rim. Remove sides and cool on wire rack; spread may be left on pan bottom.

Topping:
Combine sour cream and mayonnaise and spread over top.

Keep refrigerated until serving. Serve with more Club Crackers.

More Across Colorado

Colorado's vast plains, rugged mountains, and grand plateaus, so magnificent in their beauty and variety, seem at times to overshadow the state's history and people. But look closely. The story of Colorado is every bit as dramatic as the physical terrain. Many peoples have helped sculpt Colorado's past: the ancestral Puebloan people, whose civilization dates back thousands of years; the Utes, who occupied the Rockies for centuries; the numerous other native peoples who lived in this region; Hispano pioneers, the state's first permanent non-Indian settlers; and the men and women who came here and built cities, dug mines, and planted farms. Colorado's natural endowment is world-renowned. But the state's history, like the land on which it unfolds, features its own breathtaking peaks and valleys, its own scenes of improbable awe and splendor.

More Across Colorado

Cheese Spread

4 cups shredded sharp cheddar
1 pound bacon, cut up and browned
1 cup slivered almonds, toasted
1 cup finely sliced green onions
1½ cups mayonnaise – **do not substitute**

Yield: about 5½ cups

Mix all ingredients thoroughly. Let stand in refrigerator for a couple of hours before serving. Serve with crackers as a spread.

Note: If you prefer the bacon crispier, add it just before serving.

Chicken Wraps with Roasted Tomato and Goat Cheese

3 large plum tomatoes, sliced
2 tablespoons olive oil, divided
salt and pepper to taste
¾ cup softened goat cheese (about 5.3 ounces)
2 tablespoons minced chervil, basil, chives, *or* cilantro
2 boneless, skinless chicken breasts (about ¾ pound)
salt and pepper to taste
4 8-inch flour tortillas
1½ cups shredded romaine lettuce

Cooking time: 40 to 55 minutes
Serves: 8

Preheat oven to 350°. Line sheet pan with foil; place tomato slices in single layer. Drizzle with 1 tablespoon oil, sprinkle with salt and pepper. Bake until slices have shriveled slightly, 30 to 45 minutes. Drain any excess juice from tomatoes.
In small bowl, combine goat cheese and herb(s) of choice.
Heat remaining oil in medium non-stick skillet over medium-high heat. Add chicken, salt and pepper and sauté for 8 to 10 minutes, turning once.
Place chicken on cutting board and let rest 5 minutes, then cut into very thin slices. To assemble, heat each tortilla for 10 seconds in microwave to soften, then place on work surface. Spread with cheese mixture, then top with lettuce, roasted tomatoes and chicken. Roll tortillas tightly, wrap in plastic wrap and chill. When ready to serve, remove from plastic and cut diagonally into 1-inch pieces.

More Across Colorado

GLENWOOD SPRINGS

Doc Holliday

In some respects, John Henry Holliday's reputation was as illusory as the cure he sought. Stricken with tuberculosis at 21, the aspiring dentist came west in 1873 and roamed from Dallas to Dodge City to Tombstone, drinking and gambling hard at every stop. After shooting up a few barrooms and dispatching a rival card shark, Doc Holliday gained renown as a prolific killer and brilliant marksman. In reality he committed perhaps four or five murders, and his wheezing and boozing made him an erratic shot. But this much was true: he was hot-tempered and reckless, a dangerous man. And a dying one. By 1887, when he moved into the Hotel Glenwood, his ravaged lungs were beyond saving. He expired within a few weeks.

"[Doc Holliday] often turned the mildest joke into a deadly insult. Before a bewildered stranger could blink, he would be facing a gunfight." Carl Green and William R. Sanford, **Doc Holliday**.

Though of dubious scientific merit, the "altitude cure" for tuberculosis had a certain logic to it: Colorado's dry, sunny climate seemed the perfect antidote for victims' fevers and coughing fits. The treatment wasn't fancy (essentially, rest and fresh air), but it surely did no harm, and it worked wonders for Colorado's economic health. From 1880 to 1900 "lungers" came west in hordes, and enough of them survived to buttress the state's labor supply and consumer markets. Later, when medical advances led to more effective treatments, many of Colorado's health resorts evolved into vacation resorts, launching the state's vital tourist trade. However ephemeral its remedial effects, the cure produced undeniably real benefits for Colorado.

More Across Colorado

Chili con Queso Dip

2 pounds browned ground beef
2 pounds cubed Velveeta cheese
16-ounce jar salsa
2 15-ounce cans chili with no beans

Cooking time: 2 hours
Serves: 12

Place all ingredients in a crock pot.
Cook on high for 2 hours.
Stir occasionally.
Serve with tortilla chips.

Creamy Dill Dip

1 cup mayonnaise
1 cup sour cream
1 tablespoon dried dill
1 tablespoon dehydrated onion
2 teaspoons Beau Monde

Serves: 8

Mix all ingredients, and refrigerate for at least 1 hour.
Serve with fresh vegetables, rye bread cubes, *or* chips.
Also good on baked potatoes.

More Across Colorado

THE ROCK THAT BURNS

The first boom

It didn't glitter like gold, but oil shale promised to be every bit as valuable. Western Colorado had huge amounts of it - the equivalent of two *trillion* barrels of oil, geologists estimated - and when World War I created a sudden pinch in the fuel supply, the rush was on. Between 1916 and 1920 speculators filed thousands of claims in and around the Piceance Basin, and 200 oil shale companies formed. However, refining oil shale was literally like wringing water from stone; the costs far exceeded the yield. As a result, this vast fortune stayed in the ground - there for the taking, yet absolutely unobtainable. By 1930, investors had seen enough of this maddening state of affairs, and the oil shale business hit rock bottom.

Oil shale experimental plant near
Rifle, c. 1949.

More Across Colorado

Cucumber Dip

½ large cucumber, peeled and chopped
½ onion, chopped
¼ to ½ teaspoon garlic salt
½ teaspoon Worcestershire sauce
drop hot pepper sauce
8-ounce package cream cheese, softened
2 tablespoons mayonnaise
dash salt

Cooking time: 10 minutes

Place cucumber in strainer and press out moisture. Blend all ingredients thoroughly. Refrigerate until well chilled. Serve with vegetables, chips or crackers. Very refreshing.

Story: My Aunt Betty wouldn't ever share her fabulous Christmas Rum Cake recipe. I served this dip at a family reunion, and she asked for the recipe. Aha – I got the cake recipe! *Margaret Greivel*

Fresh Fruit Salsa

2 medium Granny Smith apples, *or* any tart
    apple
1 cup strawberries, hulled
1 kiwi, peeled
zest of 1 small orange
juice of 1 small orange
2 tablespoons brown sugar
2 tablespoons apple jelly
cinnamon graham crackers

Peel, core and chop apples.
Chop strawberries and kiwi.
Combine prepared fruit, orange zest, orange juice, brown sugar and apple jelly in 2-quart bowl.
Chill and serve with cinnamon graham crackers.

More Across Colorado

WHITE RIVER UTES

Attack at White River

Nathan C. Meeker

Nathan C. Meeker, U.S. Indian agent at the White River Agency, wanted the Utes to become Christians and farmers. But in September 1879 they were too preoccupied with hunger to care. The previous winter had been hard, and the government had not delivered on promised food supplies. Starvation stalked the Ute villages. Meeker, on the other hand, paid little attention to food. Instead, he plowed up the tribe's sacred horse track. When they objected, he asked for the Army's protection. On September 29, 1879, the Utes responded to the threat of military action. At the Agency, they killed Meeker and eleven other white men and took Meeker's wife and daughter captive. Coloradans shouted, "The Utes Must Go!" Two years later, the Tabeguache and White River Utes were removed to barren reservations in Utah.

Battle at Milk Creek

On September 29, 1879 - the same day Utes attacked the White River Agency - 120 troopers under the command of Maj. Thomas T. Thornburgh splashed across Milk Creek, a stream which marked the northern boundary of the Ute Reservation. Thornburgh had been told by Ute leaders that to cross Milk Creek meant war. Nevertheless, he deployed his men. The Utes immediately attacked, raking the soldiers with heavy fire. A week later, when the Ninth Cavalry (the famed African American Buffalo Soldiers) and the Fifth Cavalry rode to the command's rescue, forty-two troopers had been wounded, and Thornburgh and ten men lay dead. Ute losses numbered twenty-three men killed. The Battle of Milk Creek was the Utes' last military stand against white encroachment.

More Across Colorado

Hot Artichoke Dip

12 ounces cream cheese, *or* 1 cup sour cream
½ cup freshly grated Parmesan cheese
1 cup mayonnaise
1 large clove garlic, minced, *or* 1 teaspoon
    garlic granules
fresh or dried dill to taste, optional
1 can artichoke hearts, drained and chopped

Cooking time: 45 to 50 minutes

Over low heat, melt cream cheese, Parmesan cheese and mayonnaise. If using the sour cream in place of the cream cheese: Blend the mayonnaise, sour cream, Parmesan cheese and proceed.
Stir in garlic; dill, if using; and artichoke hearts. Pour into glass – *not metal* – baking dish and sprinkle with additional Parmesan cheese.
Bake at 350° until brown, hot and bubbly.
Serve warm with vegetables, crackers or tortilla chips.

Hummus

4 to 8 cloves garlic
2 1.3-pound cans garbanzo beans (chickpeas),
    rinsed, drained and rinsed
⅔ cup tahini (sesame paste), well stirred
⅓ cup olive oil
¼ cup freshly squeezed lemon juice
1 teaspoon kosher salt
water for thinning to desired consistency – only
    if needed
pita bread, *or* pita chips

Serves: 9 to 10

Drop each clove of garlic into a food processor, while the blades are spinning – this will mince the garlic.
Stop the food processor, and add the first can of garbanzo beans. Pulse the processor until the beans begin to form a smooth paste, and then add the second can, continuing the pulsing action. Slowly add the tahini and olive oil, while the processor is in a continuous spinning mode.
Add the lemon juice and salt.
If the mixture is too thick for dipping, slowly incorporate some water until it is of the desired consistency.

More Across Colorado

MOUNTAIN MEN

Jim Beckwourth

Jim Beckwourth

"We had formed the opinion . . . that Captain Beckwourth was a rough, illiterate backwoodsman, but we were most agreeably surprised to find him a polished gentleman, possessing a fund of general information which few can boast." *Rocky Mountain News*, December 1, 1859.

The boundless West could barely contain Jim Beckwourth. Born into slavery, then released by his white father, he came to the Rockies in 1824 and trapped the streams of Colorado and Wyoming with such mountain masters as Thomas Fitzpatrick, Jedediah Smith, and Jim Bridger. For forty years Beckwourth crisscrossed the wilderness as a trapper, scout, and businessman, making and witnessing history. He lived among the Crows as a war chief, helped establish El Pueblo on the Arkansas River, rode with the U.S. Army during the Mexican War, turned up in California on the eve of the Gold Rush, and operated one of Denver's first trading posts. Universally respected, Beckwourth never ceased his roaming. The life of this former slave is a monument to freedom.

More Across Colorado

Mexican Caviar Dip

2 4½-ounce cans chopped ripe olives
2 4-ounce cans diced green chiles
2 tomatoes, peeled and chopped
3 green onions, sliced
2 garlic cloves, mashed
3 tablespoons olive oil
2 teaspoons red wine vinegar
1 teaspoon pepper
dash of seasoning salt

Optional ingredients:
¼ cup chopped cilantro
1 small jalapeño pepper, seeded, de-veined, very finely chopped

Mix all ingredients and chill.
Serve with corn chips.

Serves: 10

Open-Faced Beef Tenderloin Sandwiches

2¼ pounds center-cut beef tenderloin
1 tablespoon vegetable oil
½ teaspoon salt
¼ teaspoon pepper
1 *or* 2 loaves Italian bread, sliced
spicy mustard, *or* dressing of choice

Cooking time: 35 minutes
Yield: 24 open-faced sandwiches

Preheat oven to 450°.
Rub beef with oil. Sprinkle with salt and pepper.
Place on rack in roasting pan, uncovered. Roast at 450° for 35 minutes, *or* to 130° internal temperature for medium rare.
Let stand 10 minutes.
Cut into thin slices and serve on Italian bread slices with spicy mustard, *or* dressing of choice.
If refrigerated, bring to room temperature before serving.

More Across Colorado

William E. Pabor

John Otto

More Across Colorado

FRUITA

Without the vision of William Pabor, Fruita might have withered on the vine. An experienced horticulturalist and town builder, Pabor founded Fruita in 1884 and worked his magic on Mesa County's agricultural potential. By 1900, the area's produce had gained international renown; consumers as far away as Paris tasted locally grown cherries, apples, pears, and peaches. After World War I, sagging prices and swarming insects forced many growers to cut down their orchards and plant other crops. By then Pabor had died, and though his dream of a fruit utopia came to naught, the town he planted continued to evolve. Today Fruita thrives as a center of agriculture, recreation, and natural history.

John Otto was as colorful and strange as the land he adored. Arriving in the Grand Valley in 1906, he became obsessed with the maze of tablelands and spires south of Fruita and Grand Junction; when not carving trails into its precipitous cliffs, he was badgering state and federal leaders to name the area a national park. Dubbed "the hermit of Monument Canyon," Otto was widely thought to be insane, but there was a method to his madness: Thanks mainly to him, the government created Colorado National Monument in 1911. He stayed on as caretaker, charging a dollar a year for his services, but repeated clashes with park officials got him fired in 1927. With that, Otto left for California; he never laid eyes on his beloved wilderness again.

Pumpkin Cheesecake Dip

8-ounce package cream cheese, softened
7-ounce jar marshmallow crème
½ cup canned pumpkin
½ teaspoon ground cinnamon
¼ teaspoon ground cinnamon
½ teaspoon ground nutmeg

Serves: 10

Mix all ingredients until well blended.
Cover and refrigerate for several hours.
Serve with assorted fruits and cookies.

Salsa

5 medium-size tomatoes, finely chopped
1 large onion, finely chopped
2 green bell peppers, finely chopped
2 or 3 jalapeño peppers (depending on taste),
     seeded, de-veined, finely chopped
¼ to ½ cup cilantro (to taste), finely minced
2 cloves garlic, minced
1 tablespoon olive oil
1 tablespoon balsamic vinegar
1 to 2 teaspoons salt (to taste)
1 tablespoon ground cumin
1 tablespoon oregano
juice of 1 lime

Combine all ingredients.
Refrigerate, covered, 2 to 3 hours, *or* overnight.
Keeps several days.
Serve as a relish or a dip.

Note: Optional additions are 1 can black beans, drained, rinsed, drained; 1 can whole corn, drained; or both beans and corn.

More Across Colorado

Paonia, c. 1904.

West Elk Loop

In the summer of 1881, Colorado pioneers Samuel Wade and Enos Hotchkiss rode across the mountains into the North Fork Valley, a Ute hunting ground that had just been opened to settlement. Wade surveyed this area, marking off future ranches and towns. When other settlers arrived, Wade opened the first store and post office in a log house. He named the new settlement Paeonia, but postal authorities changed the spelling to Paonia (pay-o-nee-a). By the early 1900s, the town boasted about 1,000 residents. Stores,

NORTH FORK VALLEY

churches, schools, hotels, and three newspaper offices lined the streets. Paonia had become the supply center for the valley's fruit growers, ranchers, and farmers - a position it holds today.

When Wade first came to the North Fork Valley, he spotted the wild thorn apples and buffalo berries growing everywhere. The climate was mild and sunny, the soil fertile. The following spring, Wade and a small party hauled a load of fruit saplings across the Black Mesa and set out the valley's first orchards. By the turn of the century, fruit-laden wagons rumbled over the dirt road to the railhead at Delta. From there, local fruit was shipped across the country. But the freezing winter of 1913 devastated the orchards, causing some fruit growers to pull up their trees. Other growers persevered, however, and today the valley is known as one of the nation's "champion fruit districts."

More Across Colorado

Southwestern Savory Cheesecake

1 cup finely crushed corn chips
3 tablespoons butter, melted
2 8-ounce packages cream cheese, softened
2 eggs
8-ounce package shredded Colby/Monterey
    Jack cheese
1 4-ounce can diced green chiles, drained
1 cup sour cream
1 cup chopped orange, *or* yellow bell pepper
½ cup green onion slices
⅓ cup chopped tomatoes
¼ cup pitted ripe olive slices

Cooking time: 45 minutes
Serves: 16 to 20

Preheat oven to 325°.

Stir together crushed corn chips and butter in small bowl; press into bottom of 9-inch spring form pan. Bake 15 minutes.

In large mixing bowl, beat the cream cheese and eggs with electric mixer at medium speed until well blended. Mix in shredded cheese and chiles; spoon over crust. Bake 30 minutes.

Spread sour cream over cheesecake. Loosen cake from rim of pan; cool before removing rim of pan. Chill.

Top with remaining ingredients just before serving. To serve, slice in very thin wedges. Can also serve with additional corn chips to scoop like a dip.

More Across Colorado

Delta County apple harvest, c. 1920.

More Across Colorado

DELTA

According to an 1888 U.S. Department of Agriculture report, western Colorado's thin soils, high altitude, and lack of rainfall rendered the region totally unfit for cultivation. The document's author apparently failed to notice the fruit orchards already proliferating in the valleys of the Gunnison and Colorado Rivers. Here, warm days and cool nights ripened sweet produce to perfection, and the mining towns south and east provided ready markets. Between 1890 and 1902, Delta County fruit took first-place honors at every state fair except one, adding gold medals at the 1893 and 1898 world's fairs. Ever since, Delta County has been a leading producer of Colorado apples, cherries, peaches, and pears.

Before the advent of rail service, Western Slope farmers had to hustle to get their harvests to market before the rot set in. But the 1882 arrival of the Denver & Rio Grande gave local planters easy access to Denver and Salt Lake City consumers, and the subsequent introduction of refrigerated railroad cars and warehouses placed both coasts within reach. Throughout the twentieth century, local agriculture became increasingly mechanized, enabling farmers to raise larger crops, and Delta sprouted a phalanx of canneries, packing houses, and food processing plants, driving the demand for homegrown produce to new heights. Today western Colorado's farms, sugar beet fields, and fruit orchards nourish a thriving regional economy.

Spinach Balls

2 10-ounce packages frozen chopped spinach,
    thawed and well drained
¾ cup melted butter
½ teaspoon salt
2 cups Pepperidge Farm herb stuffing mix
4 eggs, beaten
½ cup Parmesan cheese
1 onion, finely chopped

Cooking time: 15 minutes

Combine ingredients and chill for 15 minutes.
Form into 1-inch balls.
Place on greased cookie sheet.

Bake at 350° for 15 minutes.

Stuffed Mushrooms

1 pound bacon
1 package cream cheese, softened
1 pound mushrooms
¼ cup butter

Cooking time: 30 minutes
Serves: 6 to 8

Fry bacon fairly crisp, then break into pieces.
Mix bacon with cream cheese. Set aside.
Break out mushroom stems, then sauté mushroom buttons in butter
– just to coat, not to color.
Stuff caps with bacon-cheese filling.
Bake on cookie sheet at 350° for about 30 minutes, until tops brown
lightly.

More Across Colorado

Josephine Roche, president of the Rocky Mountain Fuel Company.

WHEN COAL WAS KING

A good friend to her employees

Josephine Roche was forty-two years old in 1928 when she gained control of the Rocky Mountain Fuel Company, the state's second-largest coal producer. The company owned the Kubler Mine nearby. At the time, most coal miners worked under horrendous conditions in an "environment of death." For a ten-hour day, they received about $2.50 in company scrip, redeemable only at high-priced company stores. They lived in squalid company camps. But Josephine Roche paid her miners $7.00 a day and saw to it they had decent houses, schools, and clinics. She was the first mine owner in Colorado to engage in collective bargaining with mine workers. Rocky Mountain Fuel Company miners repaid the woman they considered their friend by producing the highest amount of coal per miner in the state.

Some 300 coal mines once operated among the orchards in the North Fork Valley. Millions of tons of coal, formed in the days of the dinosaurs, lie deep beneath this valley floor. The first settlers chipped coal out of the earth to heat cabins and stores and run blacksmith forges. Soon so-called wagon mines run by one or two miners began supplying coal. The arrival of the Denver & Rio Grande Railroad in 1902 spurred the development of larger mines, including the nearby Somerset, which eventually reached five miles into the mountainside and covered 12½ square miles underground. Although competition from natural gas ended the coal boom, deposits here remain one of the nation's greatest natural resources.

More Across Colorado

Taco Dip

16-ounce can refried beans
8-ounce package cream cheese, softened
4 teaspoons Homemade Taco Seasoning Mix,
     or 1.25-ounce taco seasoning packet
2 garlic cloves, pressed
1 small tomato, chopped
¼ cup chopped onion
½ cup chopped black olives
2 tablespoons fresh chopped cilantro, *or* parsley
½ cup shredded cheddar cheese
sour cream, optional

Preheat oven to 375°.
Spread refried beans on bottom of a deep baking dish.
Combine cream cheese and taco seasoning mix in a medium-size bowl.
Add garlic to cream cheese mixture; spread over beans.
Chop tomato, onion, cilantro *or* parsley, and olives and sprinkle over cream cheese mixture. Top with cheese.
Bake for 25 to 30 minutes, or until hot.
Garnish with sour cream, if desired.
Serve with your favorite chips.

Cooking time: 25 to 30 minutes
Serves: 8 to 10

Homemade Taco Seasoning Mix

2 tablespoons chili powder
5 teaspoons paprika
4½ teaspoons cumin
1 tablespoon onion powder
2½ teaspoons garlic powder
¼ teaspoon cayenne pepper

Yield: 21 teaspoons (½ cup)

Combine all ingredients and mix well. Seal in a tight container and store in a dry place.
Note: 7 teaspoons = 2.5 ounces, the amount of a commercial packet. These packaged mixes can be expensive, and this is a practical alternative. This salt-free mix can be used in any recipe that traditionally uses the purchased taco seasoning mix.

More Across Colorado

President Theodore Roosevelt (right) on a hunting trip in Colorado, c. January 1901.

THEODORE ROOSEVELT

Colorado owes much to President Theodore Roosevelt. Sportsman and early conservationist, Roosevelt was at home camping, fishing, and hunting in the solitude of the western wilderness. On several occasions in the early 1900s, he came to the West Elk region to hunt deer and bear. If the nation were to prosper, he believed, it must conserve its natural resources - timber, minerals, watersheds, ranges, and wildlife. Despite opposition from Congress and large corporations, Roosevelt added 86 million acres to the national forest system, bringing the total forest lands to 151 million acres. In doing so, he affirmed the importance of protecting public lands and established the climate in which primitive wilderness areas, such as West Elk, could later be set aside.

Toasted Almonds

1 pound shelled raw almonds
1 tablespoon sea salt
water

Cooking time: 8 to 10 hours
Yield: 4 cups

Cover almonds with water. Add sea salt and stir well. Let almonds soak for 8 hours. Drain, rinse and drain. Pat dry with paper towels. Spread over cookie sheets. Bake at 200° to 220° (no higher) for 8 to 10 hours until toasted and crunchy.

Note: Almonds prepared in this manner are easier to digest because the enzyme inhibitors present in nuts are broken.

Vidalia Onion Dip

2 tablespoons peanut oil
2 tablespoons unsalted butter
2 large Vidalia onions, *or* other available sweet
    onions, chopped
1 cup sour cream
1 cup mayonnaise
1 teaspoon crushed red pepper flakes
½ teaspoon salt
¼ teaspoon ground red pepper (cayenne)
⅛ teaspoon red pepper sauce

Cooking time: 40 to 45 minutes
Serves: 10

Heat oil and butter in large, non-stick skillet over medium heat. Add onions; reduce heat to low.
Slowly cook until onions are caramelized, for 40 to 45 minutes. Remove from heat; let cool.
In medium bowl, combine remaining ingredients. Stir in onions. Chill.
Serve with chips.

More Across Colorado

The hanging flume of Dolores Canyon.

HANGING FLUME

In need of water to work its Dolores Canyon gold claims, the Montrose Placer Mining Company built a thirteen-mile canal and flume to deliver water from the San Miguel River. The last five miles of the flume clung to the wall of the canyon itself, running along the cliff face. Constructed between 1888 and 1891, the four-foot-deep, five-foot-four-inch-wide "hanging flume" carried 23,640,000 gallons of water in a twenty-four-hour period. Its construction dazzled mining pros with its sheer ingenuity. The placer claim, unfortunately, dazzled no one; after three years of indifferent yields the company folded, abandoning the flume to the ravages of weather and time. Now listed on the National Register of Historic Places, this engineering marvel symbolizes the twists of fate so often encountered in the pursuit of Rocky Mountain gold.

More Across Colorado

Apple Loaf Bread

*For best flavor and ease of slicing, day-ahead preparation is recommended. ***

½ cup butter
1 cup sugar
2 eggs
1 teaspoon vanilla extract
2 cups flour
¼ teaspoon salt
1 teaspoon baking soda
1 teaspoon baking powder
2 tablespoons milk
2 cups peeled and finely chopped apples –
     Braeburns are good, but any variety is
     fine

Cooking time: 1 hour
Yield: 1 loaf

Miriam Graetzer
Quilt House Bed & Breakfast
Estes Park, Colorado

In large mixing bowl, combine butter and sugar. Beat until creamy; add eggs and vanilla and beat thoroughly.

Whisk together 1 cup of the flour, the salt, baking soda and baking powder. Add to butter mixture along with the milk. Mix thoroughly.

Place second cup of flour on top of batter. Spoon apples on top of flour. Gently coat apples with flour. Stir mixture gently to completely moisten the flour. Mixture will be thick.

Oil a loaf pan on bottom and up the sides. Spoon in the mixture. Smooth the top, then make a light indentation in the center with the back of a spoon.

Bake at 350° for 1 hour.

Loaf is done when it shrinks from pan sides and a toothpick inserted in center comes out clean. Place on wire rack 10 minutes to cool, then remove from pan to rack to complete cooling.

* The flavor is enhanced the second day, and the loaf slices better too, but if you can't wait, let it cool and enjoy.

More Across Colorado

Sheep camp

More Across Colorado

SHEEP-CATTLE WARS

"Thirty-eight hundred sheep were stampeded over a bluff into Parachute Creek on September 10th. . . . One of the herders, Carl Brown, resisted and was shot in the hip." *Craig Courier*, September 14, 1894.

When forty armed cattlemen ordered him to stop grazing his sheep in northwestern Colorado, Jack Edwards spat, "This is public domain, and I have as much right to use it as anybody!" The law agreed with him, but his captors had tradition - and guns - on their side. By local custom, whoever first grazed a section of open range held "rights" to it; sheepherders were considered trespassers and treated accordingly. In the 1890s and again in the 1910s, the cowmen terrorized their rivals, clubbing sheep to death and shooting defiant herders. The sheepmen countered by buying or leasing private acreage. Peace finally came in 1934, when Congress passed the Taylor Grazing Act, which imposed strict grazing regulations. By then Jack Edwards had retired, a wealthy stockman - in Oregon.

Banana Oatmeal Bread

1 cup butter
2 cups sugar
2½ cups flour
2 cups Quick oatmeal
4 eggs
2½ cups mashed bananas (about 4 bananas)
1 cup chopped nuts, optional
½ teaspoon salt
1 teaspoon baking powder
1 teaspoon vanilla extract

Cooking time: 1 hour
Yield: 2 loaves

Grease two 9.2 x 5.2 x 2.7-inch loaf pans.
Combine all ingredients in one bowl.
Divide batter between the pans.
Bake at 350° for 1 hour or until a toothpick comes out clean.

Note: This is the fastest, moistest, easiest bread you'll ever make – and it freezes great.

More Across Colorado

Ann Bassett

BROWN'S HOLE

Women of Brown's Hole

As the unlikely head of her own gang, Elizabeth Bassett combined Old South gentility with raw frontier courage. Neighbors and ranch hands basked in her generous hospitality, but good manners only went so far in Brown's Hole. Bassett backed down from no one in this valley full of coarse characters, doing whatever was necessary to ensure her family's well-being. Her two daughters were just as fearless. Ann Bassett, dubbed "queen of the cattle rustlers," defied prosecutors and murderous rivals who tried to run her out of Brown's Hole. Her sister, Josie, built a homestead in Utah and worked it independently for half a century. She was still chopping her own wood at the age of eighty.

More Across Colorado

Bran Refrigerator Rolls

This recipe calls for day-ahead preparation.*

1 package dry yeast
½ cup lukewarm water
½ cup solid shortening
6 tablespoons sugar
½ cup boiling water
¾ teaspoon salt
½ cup All-Bran cereal
1 egg
3 to 3¼ cups all-purpose flour
oil for brushing dough

Cooking time: 12 to 15 minutes
Yield: 18 to 24 rolls

Add dry yeast to lukewarm water and stir slightly to blend. Set aside to soften yeast.

Cream shortening and sugar thoroughly. Add boiling water, salt and All-Bran. Cool to lukewarm, then add the egg and softened yeast and mix well. Stir in enough flour to make a soft dough; dough will stiffen somewhat as it stands. Place dough in a well-greased bowl; brush top of dough lightly with oil and cover tightly.

*Store in refrigerator overnight.

When ready to use dough, preheat oven to 400°.

Shape rolls as desired and place in greased pan or muffin tins. Brush tops with oil and cover with a towel. Let rise in warm place until almost double in bulk, about 1½ hours.

Bake at 400° for 12 to 15 minutes. Serve warm and enjoy.

Note: These make nice cloverleaf rolls by rolling dough in lightly floured hands into uniform balls and placing 3 balls in a 2½-inch or 3-inch muffin cup.

More Across Colorado

Fremont rock art, Dinosaur National Monument.

MARKS OF HUMAN PASSAGE

The Fremont

Aside from some dwellings and scattered artifacts, the ancient people of northwestern Colorado did not leave much behind - certainly nothing as dramatic as the Anasazi cliff dwellings. Yet the Fremont, as these loosely related groups are known, lived in that region for hundreds of years with a surprising degree of comfort. The first Native Americans appeared as early as 2,000 years ago, but around AD 200 the Fremont began building log-and-mud houses, planting corn, beans, and squash, and developing sophisticated arts and tools. After AD 1200 they apparently abandoned the region - perhaps in search of a more hospitable climate, or perhaps to avoid competition from nomadic peoples entering the region.

Brown Sugar Oatmeal Muffins

1 cup Old Fashioned oats
½ cup whole wheat flour
½ cup all-purpose flour
2 teaspoons baking powder
½ teaspoon salt
2 large eggs
¾ cup packed dark brown sugar
¾ cup milk
¼ cup melted butter, *or* oil
1 teaspoon vanilla extract

Cooking time: 20 minutes
Yield: 24 muffins

Preheat oven to 400°.
Mix oats, flours, baking powder and salt in large bowl; set aside.
In small bowl, whisk together eggs and brown sugar until smooth.
Whisk in milk, melted butter *or* oil, and vanilla.
Pour liquid mixture over dry ingredients.
Fold in with a rubber spatula just until dry ingredients are moistened.
Scoop batter into 24 greased *or* paper-lined, 2½-inch muffin tins.
Bake at 400° for 15 to 20 minutes, until centers are springy to touch. Remove to wire rack and cool.

More Across Colorado

Excavating a site near Yellow Jacket, c. 1975.

ANCIENT VALLEY CULTURES

Their homes may now be less visible than the cliff dwellings of their Mesa Verde neighbors, but the ancient farmers of southwestern Colorado were far more numerous. By the twelfth century, perhaps 12,000 people tilled the green canyons and plateaus of the Montezuma Valley, raising beans, squash, and corn. They lived in underground structures and, later, masonry pueblos; and they crafted fine stone tools, elegant pottery, and intricate baskets. Then, for several reasons - perhaps a long period of drought, perhaps the threat of hostile neighbors, perhaps depletion of natural resources - they left their villages around AD 1300. Archaeologists believe many of them migrated south, establishing new settlements, or joining existing ones, that gave rise to modern-day Pueblo culture.

More Across Colorado

Butterhorn Croissant Rolls

This recipe calls for day-ahead preparation. *

1 tablespoon dry yeast
¼ cup warm water
½ cup sugar
3 eggs, beaten
½ cup butter
4 cups flour, plus up to ½ cup more
¾ cup milk
½ teaspoon salt
oil for brushing

Cooking time: 10 to 12 minutes
Yield: 24 rolls

Dissolve yeast in water. Add sugar and eggs. Add remaining ingredients and mix well with wooden spoon. Let rise until double.
Punch down and refrigerate until ready to make rolls.
* *Do the above the day or evening before baking.*

Next day, preheat oven to 350°. D
Divide dough into thirds. Roll each third into a circle and cut into 8 wedges. Roll each wedge from the wide end to the small end. Place onto greased cookie sheet and curve into croissant shape. Brush with oil. Cover with plastic wrap and let rise 1 to 1½ hours or until double in bulk.
Bake at 350° for 10 to 12 minutes or until golden brown.

Note: To hasten dough, use 2 tablespoons yeast and do not refrigerate dough.

Story: My family is from Texas and we love pecans. We place chopped pecans onto rolled-out dough prior to rolling up each croissant. *Nancy Parma*

More Across Colorado

DRYLAND FARMING

The first workable system for farming Colorado's dry southwestern plateau emerged some 2,000 years ago. Over the next twelve centuries, farmers gradually developed a series of techniques - water storage, plant breeding, precise planting cycles and, beginning around 900, check-dam irrigation - to coax crops from the desert. What they couldn't control through technology, they sought to influence through ritual and prayer. These early farmers planted smaller fields and reaped thinner harvests than their modern-day counterparts, but the magnitude of their accomplishments cannot be overestimated. In addition to building the first settlements in present-day Colorado, they perfected a model for dryland farming.

Even with this technology of the twenty-first century, this is not an easy land to master. Surviving with *first*-century technology required toughness, ingenuity, and faith. The extremes of temperature and scarcity of water helped shape the culture of ancient populations; they, in turn, brought their culture to bear on the land. From the sixth century on, local populations farmed extensively, and by the tenth century their small check-dams and reservoirs provided water to help make these acres fertile. They also developed weaving and yucca ropes, and they crafted turquoise jewelry. Throughout the period they conducted a brisk trade with neighbors to acquire whatever the earth or their inventiveness could not provide. What little they had to work with, these primeval pioneers worked to perfection - they survived in this harsh land for more than one thousand years.

Black and white pottery near Cortez, dating between AD 900 and 1100.

More Across Colorado

Cheddar Pecan Scones

*For best results, freeze before baking. ***

Full recipe:
10 cups flour
5 tablespoons baking powder
2½ teaspoons salt
½ cup sugar
3¾ cups butter, cold
4 cups cream
10 eggs
4 cups sharp cheddar cheese
4 cups pecans chopped
cream and sugar

One-fourth of recipe:
2½ cups flour
4 tablespoons baking powder
¾ teaspoon salt
⅛ cup sugar
1 cup (2 sticks) butter, cold
1 cup cream
2 eggs plus 1 egg white
1 cup sharp cheddar cheese
1 cup pecans chopped
cream and sugar

Mix dry ingredients and butter until mealy.
Add cream and eggs just to blend. **Do not overmix.**
Add cheese and pecans. Roll to ¾-inch thickness on floured surface and cut into triangles. Freeze on waxed paper-lined cookie sheet, then put into storage bags for freezing until ready to bake.
* *For best results, freezing is recommended before baking.*

Frozen scones will keep for 4 months. When ready to serve, remove desired number from freezer. Brush frozen scones with cream and sprinkle with enough sugar to cover.
Bake at 425° for 7 to 10 minutes, or until lightly browned. May be served with your favorite fruit preserves.

Cooking time: 7 to 10 minutes
Yield: full recipe, 100 to 150 small scones
        one-fourth recipe, about 25 scones

James Finnerty, Director
Governor's Residence
Denver, Colorado

More Across Colorado

THE UTES

The Utes, Colorado's oldest inhabitants, have lived here at least a thousand years, perhaps forever. Certainly they have been here since the state's recorded history began; the earliest Spanish explorers found them in possession of the Central Rockies in the seventeenth century. They were one of the first tribes to acquire horses, and they used this advantage to broaden their territory and strengthen their claim upon it. By the early eighteenth century the Utes held everything from the Utah deserts to the plains of eastern Colorado. Skilled warriors and formidable defenders, they repelled all intruders until the late 1800s, when the lure of gold and silver brought American settlers in force. Outnumbered and outgunned, the Utes saw their vast domain reduced to two small reservations in Colorado and one in Utah.

Though dressed up as a land-reform measure, the 1887 Dawes Act was nothing less than an attempt at cultural genocide. The law sought to destroy the unity of Indian tribes by breaking their reservations into individually owned 160-acre farms, or allotments. The Southern Utes resisted until 1895, when a tribal referendum on the issue passed by just five votes. With sentiment so evenly divided, the Utes decided to split their territory. Those who opposed allotment moved to the western half of the reservation, which remained collectively owned and became known as the Ute Mountain Ute Reservation. Allotment proceeded on the Southern Ute Reservation, but the people there remained a tribe, unified despite the splintering of their landhold. Ultimately, the Dawes Act rested on a faulty premise - that Indians should be remade in the white man's image.

When the question of allotment arose, the Mouache, Capote, and Weenuche bands divided over the issue. The Weenuche, under guidance from Ignacio (standing left), chose not to accept allotments, and they settled on the Ute Mountain Ute reservation. Buckskin Charlie's (seated) and Severo's (standing right) bands divided their lands into allotments - hence the checkerboard quality of the Southern Ute reservation.

More Across Colorado

Cinnamon Streusel Coffee Cake

Streusel ingredients:
3 tablespoons flour
3 tablespoons melted butter
3 teaspoons cinnamon
¾ cup brown sugar
¾ cup chopped pecans

Coffee cake ingredients:
½ cup shortening, *or* butter
1½ cups sugar
2 eggs
2¼ cups flour
½ teaspoon salt
2 teaspoons baking powder
½ teaspoon baking soda
1 cup buttermilk
1 teaspoon vanilla extract

Cooking time: 40 minutes
Serves: 8

Combine the streusel ingredients and set aside.

Grease an 11x16-inch baking pan. Blend shortening, *or* butter, and sugar until fluffy.

Add eggs. Beat on low speed until combined.

Add dry ingredients and buttermilk alternately to the beaten mixture.

Beat on low speed after each addition until combined.

Stir in the vanilla. Spread half of batter in prepared pan.

Sprinkle half of streusel mixture on top of batter.

Add remaining batter, then top with remaining streusel.

Bake at 350° for 40 minutes.

More Across Colorado

Petroglyphs

THE FOUR CORNERS

The term Four Corners dates to 1868, when new territorial demarcations created America's lone quad-state conjunction. But nations intersected in this region hundreds of years before those boundaries were drawn. In the seventeenth century the four cornerstones were the Spanish, the Utes, the Navajos, and the Apaches; descendants of all are still here today. With its severe climate and rugged terrain, the Four Corners region possesses a powerful mystique; as recently as the 1870s portions of the area had never been seen by non-Indians. Though mining, tourism, and agriculture all left their mark during the twentieth century, the Four Corners remains imbued with a sense of the eternal. It is one of North America's most spectacular places, a land of unparalleled beauty and a rich cultural history.

Delicious Parker House Rolls

2 packages dry yeast
½ cup warm water
1 tablespoon sugar
2 cups lukewarm milk
1 cup warm water
3 large fresh eggs, room temperature
½ cup oil
½ cup sugar
4 pounds all-purpose flour, plus more for work
    surface
2 teaspoons salt
cooking spray, *or* oil
melted butter

Cooking time: 20 minutes
Yield: 4 dozen rolls

Combine yeast, warm water and sugar.
Let sit for 10 to 15 minutes, then place in very large bowl.
Add milk plus warm water, eggs, oil, sugar, most of the flour and all of the salt.
Mix. Add flour a bit at a time until dough is soft and pliable. Use a mixer with a bread hook if you have one.
Place on floured surface and knead until dough is not sticky.
Place in a large bowl.
Spray with cooking spray or brush with oil.
Let rise for at least 1 hour in a warm place.
Punch down and place on floured surface.
Roll to ¾-inch thickness.
Butter entire surface with melted butter.
Cut out with a 3-inch round cookie cutter and fold over each round in half. Butter and allow to rise for about 1 hour.
Bake at 400° for 20 minutes, then butter tops of rolls.

More Across Colorado

Ouray and Chipeta in Washington, D.C., in 1880, six months before Ouray's death.

CHIPETA (1843 - 1924)

She was born a Kiowa Apache but raised a Tabeguache Ute. In 1859, she married Ouray, and the two of them became inseparable. Photographs of Chipeta reveal a woman who appears utterly serene and at peace with herself. The historical record speaks of her dignity, her devotion to husband and family, and her attention to the needs of others. Like Ouray, she apparently moved easily among whites, who spoke glowingly of her beauty and "queenly" demeanor. When Ouray died in 1880, Chipeta was forced to leave the farm and take up life with other Tabeguache Utes on the bleak reservation lands of eastern Utah, where she died in 1924. Her remains were moved to the farm she loved.

Ouray and Chipeta's farm

Ouray and Chipeta settled in the Uncompahgre Valley sometime in the 1860s. When the Los Pinos Agency moved to this valley in 1875, Ouray was already working a 500-acre farm, and living in a six-room adobe house. This house Ouray and Chipeta filled with chairs, iron beds, silverware and china, a piano, and they even hired a Hispanic servant, who answered the ring of a silver bell and drove a fancy carriage. All this was in the vain hope that by showing government officials that Utes were capable of adapting to white ways, their people might escape reservation life and retain their Western Slope homeland.

Lemon Blueberry Bread

2 cups flour
1½ teaspoons baking powder
¼ teaspoon salt
½ cup oil
1 cup sugar
2 eggs
⅓ cup milk
½ cup chopped walnuts
2 teaspoons grated lemon zest
1 cup blueberries

Glaze:
¼ cup lemon juice
⅓ cup sugar

Cooking time: 1 hour and 10 minutes
Yield: 1 loaf

Mix first 7 ingredients in bowl until just mixed.
Fold in walnuts, lemon zest and blueberries.
Pour into greased loaf pan.
Bake at 350° for 1 hour and 10 minutes, or until knife inserted in center comes out clean.
Let cool 10 minutes and remove from pan onto wire rack.

Glaze:
Heat lemon juice and sugar until sugar is dissolved. Pour glaze over loaf.

More Across Colorado

Otto Mears, 1870s.

"Pathfinder of the San Juans"

In addition to designing the roads that opened the San Juan Mountains to settlement, Otto Mears helped engineer the 1873 Brunôt Treaty, which transferred this remote wilderness from Ute to U.S. sovereignty. A government Indian agent and fluent Ute speaker, Mears made important contributions to the agreement and used his influence to ensure the tribe's approval. The wave of miners and ranchers unleashed by the cession arrived almost exclusively via Mears's marvelously conceived toll roads, which traversed 450 miles of Colorado's most difficult terrain. In 1891 he launched the Rio Grande Southern Railroad, whose depot in Placerville became the shipping center for the San Miguel Basin and Paradox Valley, to the point that between 1907 and 1909 it was one of the world's busiest cattle shipping points. A self-educated Russian Jewish immigrant, Mears succeeded at almost everything he tried. His giant footprints still crisscross the San Juans; most of the region's highways today follow routes he pioneered.

More Across Colorado

Nutty Yeast Rolls

*Dough may be refrigerated overnight. *

Dough:
4½ cups flour
1 package rapid-rise dry yeast
½ teaspoon salt
½ cup milk
1 cup butter
½ cup sugar
2 eggs

Filling:
4 cups finely chopped walnuts
½ cup milk
1 cup sugar

Cooking time: 18 to 20 minutes
Yield: 4 dozen rolls

In a mixer bowl, combine 2 cups of the flour, yeast and salt. In a saucepan, over low heat (115° to 120°), warm milk, butter and sugar, stirring until butter is melted.
Add warm liquid to dry flour mixture.
Mix until well blended. Add eggs and mix again.
Stir in remaining 2½ cups of flour, one cup at a time.
Dough will be moderately soft; it will ball up, yet still be sticky.
Divide dough into 6 balls. Cover and allow to rest for 10 minutes.
* Dough may be refrigerated overnight at this point.

Mix walnuts, milk and sugar to form a spreadable mixture for the filling.
On a thoroughly floured surface, roll out one ball of dough at a time to form a ⅛-inch-thick rectangle.
Spread ⅔ of filling mixture evenly on dough.
Gently roll dough lengthwise to form a long roll.
Using a sharp knife, slice into 1-inch sections.
Place slices on cookie sheets and bake at 350° for 18 to 20 minutes.

More Across Colorado

Built in 1933, the Galloping Goose #5 transported light freight and mail through 1949. With the loss of the mail contract, she carried tourists until 1951. Today, the restored #5 is housed at the Dolores Visitors Center.

THE GALLOPING GOOSE

After sinking to the brink of bankruptcy in 1931, the Rio Grande Southern Railroad took flight again on the unlikely wings of the Galloping Goose. This unique vehicle, hatched from spare parts by Placerville mechanic Jack Odenbaugh, fused train wheels and a freight car to an automobile chassis; the resulting hybrid seated a dozen or so passengers and towed several tons of mail and cargo. Curious tourists flocked to the Goose, while shippers enjoyed favorable rates and flexible service. It proved so successful that the railroad sidetracked all conventional trains after 1933 and ran entirely on Goose power; eventually there were seven "geese" traveling the tracks. Efficient and lightweight, the Goose foreshadowed the rise of the trucking industry - which, ironically, made this strange bird obsolete after World War II. Though permanently grounded in 1950, the Galloping Goose retains a special place in American railroading history.

Pineapple Bread

3½ cups flour
4 teaspoons baking powder
½ teaspoon baking soda
1 teaspoon salt
1½ cups nutmeats
6 tablespoons butter, softened
1½ cups brown sugar, packed
2 eggs
2 cups canned crushed pineapple, including
    juice

Topping:
4 tablespoons sugar
1 teaspoon cinnamon

Cooking time: 50 to 60 minutes
Yield: 2 loaves

Butter 2 loaf pans.
Whisk together flour, baking powder, baking soda and salt.
Stir nuts into flour mixture.
In a separate bowl, cream butter and brown sugar.
Beat in eggs.
Stir in half of flour mixture, using a spoon.
Stir in pineapple.
Add remaining flour.
Divide the batter between pans.

Topping:
Combine sugar and cinnamon and sprinkle on top of batter.
Bake at 350° for 50 to 60 minutes.
Cool for 5 minutes before removing from pans.

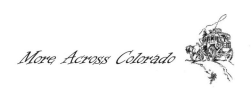

More Across Colorado

THE SOUTHERN UTES

The Utes traditionally lived in seven distinct bands, each with its own territory and leaders. The pressure of white settlement shattered this confederation: The four northern bands were sent to a Utah reservation in 1881, while the three southern bands - the Weenuche, Capote, and Mouache - remained in Colorado. Forced by government policies to take up farming, adopt Christianity, and send their children to English-only boarding schools, the Southern Utes by 1930 were struggling to maintain their identity. But the Indian Reorganization Act of 1934 provided new hope. Since then, the Southern Utes have established an elected tribal council and developed profitable agriculture, tourism, gaming, and natural gas industries. More important, they have rekindled traditional ceremonies such as the Bear Dance and made great progress toward preserving their language and history.

Southern Utes at a festival in Boulder, Colorado, 1909. Buckskin Charlie is standing at center; his wife, Emma, is seated third from left; and his son, Antonio Buck, Sr., is standing third from left. After Buckskin Charlie's death, his son became the last hereditary chief of the Southern Utes. Today, the positions of chairman and tribal council are elective.

More Across Colorado

Pumpkin Bread

29-ounce can pumpkin
3 cups sugar
1½ cups oil
1⅓ cups water
4 eggs
5¼ cups flour
1 tablespoon baking soda
1½ teaspoons salt
1½ teaspoons cinnamon
1½ teaspoons nutmeg
1½ teaspoons ginger
1 cup chopped walnuts, optional

Cooking time: 60 to 75 minutes
Yield: 3 loaves

Grease three 9x5-inch loaf pans.
In large bowl, blend first 5 ingredients.
Beat 1 minute at medium speed.
Add remaining ingredients.
Blend at low speed until moistened.
Beat 1 minute at medium speed.
Fold in nuts if using.
Pour batter into prepared pans.
Bake at 350° for 60 to 75 minutes, or until breads test done.
Cool for 5 minutes.
Remove from pans. Cool on wire racks.

More Across Colorado

HARD ROCK RESILIENCY

San Juan mines were the first to use aerial tramways to help overcome the cost of freighting, bad weather, and high elevations. Trams often served as conveyances for the miners too, as seen in this photo, c. 1895.

More Across Colorado

Was there ever a tougher, more stouthearted worker than the nineteenth-century miner? He spent up to twelve hours a day, six days a week underground, drilling holes into solid rock, filling them with explosives, blasting the stone into rubble, and hefting the pieces into ore cars. His tools evolved over time: Mechanical drills replaced the hammer and hand steel, electric lamps supplanted candles and carbide lamps, and aerial trams took over for some mule-drawn wagons. But the miseries and perils of the job remained constant: The tight, dimly lit spaces; the dust that suffused his lungs (and, in many cases, eventually killed him); the ever-present threat of a cave-in. He earned better wages in the mines ($3 to $4 a day) than he probably could elsewhere. But he laid his life on the line every day.

"Instant Cities"

In the last quarter of the nineteenth century, towns came and went in the San Juan Mountains as abruptly as gusts of wind. A promising mineral strike might spawn a complete settlement - houses, a general store, saloons, and all - almost overnight. But disappointing yields, faltering mineral prices, an inaccessible location, a fire, a hard winter, or a richer strike elsewhere could (and usually did) empty the place out just as quickly. Despite the pitfalls, people kept building these "instant cities," hauling printing presses and milling machinery to the unlikeliest places, opening banks and erecting hotels, certain that *their* town was blessed with some special destiny. Most, alas, were destined to bust. But their remnants, still hidden throughout the San Juans, bear powerful witness to the enterprising spirit and optimism of the frontier.

Pumpkin Muffins

2½ cups oatmeal
2 cups flour
1½ cups brown sugar
2 teaspoons baking powder
1 teaspoon cinnamon
1 teaspoon baking soda
1 teaspoon nutmeg
1 teaspoon salt
2 teaspoons vanilla extract
2 eggs, slightly beaten
2 cups canned pumpkin
1 cup oil
½ cup milk

Cooking time: 15 to 20 minutes
Yield: 24 to 30 muffins

Grease 24 to 30 muffin cups, or use cupcake liners.
Combine dry ingredients.
Add remaining ingredients, stirring only until moistened.
Fill muffin cups three-quarters full.
Bake at 400° for 15 to 20 minutes.

Frances Owens
Colorado's First Lady
Office of the First Lady
136 State Capitol
Denver, Colorado

More Across Colorado

Cliff Palace, dating between A.D. 1100 and 1300.

More Across Colorado

ANCESTRAL PUEBLOANS

We know southwestern Colorado's ancestral people by their impressive handiwork. Their dwellings, evolving from tiny pithouses to the sprawling cliff manors of Mesa Verde, inspire wonder today; their roads and ditches survive, albeit as faint desert scratches; their ceramic pots and decorative baskets grace museums throughout the Four Corners region. Kivas, pipes, pictographs, petroglyphs, flutes, and other remains hint at the nature of their passions and beliefs, but we still don't know for certain where these prolific builders came from, nor why they left after 1,300 years of residence. Most researchers think they migrated south, blending with local populations to form the modern-day Pueblo cultures of New Mexico and Arizona. Archaeologists continue to accumulate and refine information that might help us to learn the origins and fate of these ancestral Coloradans.

The thousand-year-old relics of Colorado's ancestral Puebloan civilization lie scattered across the Ute Mountain Ute Reservation. The Utes traditionally avoided these sites and whatever spirits might attend them, but in 1961 tribal chief Jack House, recognizing their cultural value and out of respect for the ancestral people, launched a campaign to protect the remains. His efforts led to the creation of Ute Mountain Ute Tribal Park, 125,000 acres of sandstone cliffs, wooded valleys, and sliver-thin canyons. Within this preserve, Ute guides conduct tours to antiquities undisturbed for centuries. The past has never truly departed from this enchanted ground; its spirit is still palpable, resting just beneath the surface of the present.

Raisin Brown Bread

1½ cups boiling water
1¼ cups raisins
1 cup sugar
1 heaping tablespoon butter, softened
1 egg
2 teaspoons baking soda
1 teaspoon vanilla
1 cup walnuts
2 cups flour

Cooking time: 50 to 60 minutes
Yield: 1 loaf

Pour boiling water over raisins and allow to cool – for as long as overnight.
Combine sugar, butter and egg.
Stir in baking soda, vanilla and nuts.
Add raisins and liquid alternately with flour.
Pour into greased 9x5-inch loaf pan.
Bake at 350° for 50 to 60 minutes.

More Across Colorado

Miners' housing, Uravan, around 1950.

"THE MAGIC METAL"

They came by the thousands, armed with Geiger counters and scintillators, in search of the "magic metal" - uranium. It was the 1950s, the era of the Cold War, and the Atomic Energy Commission was purchasing uranium. Anyone might become a "uranium-aire." Said one prospector, "We slid down canyons and toiled up steep inclines where the mules had to scramble to keep their footing." Eventually, 200 uranium mines honeycombed the Uravan area. Miners lived in canvas tents and tarpaper shacks that clung to the mesas. All supplies, food, and water had to be hauled in. By 1960 the uranium boom was over. For the next three decades, the mines continued to produce uranium. However, most of the mined mineral no longer went toward the production of nuclear weapons, but rather as fuel for nuclear power plants.

More Across Colorado

Rhubarb Bread

1⅓ cups brown sugar
⅔ cup vegetable oil
1 beaten egg
1 teaspoon vanilla extract
1 cup buttermilk or sour milk
2½ cups all-purpose flour
¾ teaspoon salt
1 teaspoon baking soda
½ teaspoon cinnamon
1½ to 2 cups fresh rhubarb, finely diced
½ cup chopped walnuts, optional

Cooking time: 35 to 45 minutes
Serves: 12

Preheat oven to 350°.
Combine sugar and oil. Blend in the egg, vanilla and milk.
In a separate bowl, combine flour, salt, baking soda and cinnamon.
Add to the moist ingredients and mix well.
Stir in rhubarb and nuts.
Divide batter between 2 well-greased, 8x4-inch loaf pans.

Bake at 350° for 35 to 45 minutes, or until tested with toothpick.

Note: Fresh rhubarb works best. If using frozen, decrease amount and drain thoroughly. Even people who don't like rhubarb love this bread, and it's a cinch to make.

More Across Colorado

Ute encampment, 1874.

AN ABUNDANT EARTH

The bountiful food resources of the Uncompahgre Valley normally allowed the Tabeguache Utes a life free from hunger. Elk and deer ranged through the valley in profusion, as did antelope, mountain sheep, beaver, sage hens, and ducks and geese; all were hunted. The valley was also rich in berries, roots, nuts, and seeds, which provided a welcome and necessary supplement to a meat-heavy diet. Berries were either eaten when picked or dried in the sun and stored for winter consumption. Yampa (or wild carrots), sunflower seeds, and piñon nuts were prized foods, too. Finally, buffalo were hunted on the great plains east of the mountains, a risky venture but one that changed Ute life.

The mountain country of present Colorado and Utah was home to the Ute Indians for hundreds, perhaps thousands, of years. Loosely divided into seven bands, the Utes called themselves the *Nuche*, or The People. Spaniards called them *Yutas*, while their great enemies, the Cheyennes, knew them as Black People. In the early 1600s, they were among the first native peoples to acquire horses from the Spanish - and life changed radically. Mounted on their swift ponies, the Utes enjoyed fabulous wealth, for now buffalo, once so hard to kill, were easy prey. Prosperous, mobile, and adaptable to new technologies, the Utes successfully defended their mountain homeland against all intruders for 300years.

More Across Colorado

Sweet Corn Bread

1 cup milk
2 eggs
½ cup butter, melted
2 tablespoons vanilla extract
2 cups Bisquick Mix
6 tablespoons yellow cornmeal
⅔ cup sugar

Cooking time: 35 minutes
Serves: 8 to 10

Blend milk, eggs, butter and vanilla.
Add Bisquick Mix, cornmeal and sugar.
Grease a 9x9-inch pan.
Pour batter into pan.
Bake at 350° for 35 minutes.

Zucchini Squash Bread

3 eggs
2 cups sugar
1 cup vegetable oil
2 cups medium zucchini, grated – *not peeled*
3 cups flour
¼ teaspoon baking powder
3 teaspoons vanilla extract
1 teaspoon each salt, baking soda and cinnamon
1 cup nuts
½ cup raisins, optional

Grease and flour 2 loaf pans.
In a large bowl, blend eggs, sugar, oil and grated squash.
Whisk all dry ingredients together and slowly add to zucchini mixture.
Pour batter in prepared pans.
Bake at 350° for 1 hour.

Cooking time: 1 hour
Yield: 2 loaves

More Across Colorado

Turntable in switchback, Silverton Railway.

More Across Colorado

RAILS INTO THE SAN JUANS

It took a special kind of railroad to negotiate the arduous terrain of the Rocky Mountains. Narrow-gauge lines, with rails spaced just three feet apart (rather than the standard four feet, eight and a half inches), allowed for the tight turns and daredevil engineering this labyrinthine landscape demanded. William Jackson Palmer's Denver & Rio Grande Railway was one of the first to introduce narrow gauge to Colorado, and he hoped the newfangled track would revolutionize the industry. It didn't, but it did transform life in mining towns such as Silverton: Freight that otherwise would have plodded along via wagons or pack mules now could roll back and forth with greater speed and efficiency. Between 1882 (when the D&RG arrived) and 1899, four narrow-gauge lines served Silverton, tying the community firmly into Colorado's commercial network.

Durango & Silverton Narrow Gauge Railroad

If not for the D&RG, Silverton might have vanished long ago. The twisting, turning, forty-five-mile spur from Durango took nine months to build. When it finally opened in July 1882, shipping rates immediately tumbled fivefold, and long-suffering residents at last enjoyed reliable access to hardware, lumber, fresh produce, and other basics. The D&RG was Silverton's lifeline until after World War II, when mine closures and the rise of auto travel nearly forced the company to abandon the branch. But breathtaking scenery made it increasingly popular as a tourist attraction in the late 1940s. Known today as the Durango & Silverton Narrow Gauge Railroad, it ranks among Colorado's best-loved vacation stops, giving nearly 200,000 passengers annually a real taste of nineteenth-century rail travel.

Breakfast Casserole

1 package Simply Potatoes, shredded
1 cup cooked breakfast sausage, ham cubes,
      crumbled bacon, *or* crab meat
3 eggs, beaten
1 teaspoon seasoning salt
½ cup milk
4 ounces Pepper Jack cheese, shredded
4 ounces cheddar cheese, shredded
salsa, optional
sour cream, optional

Cooking time: 45 minutes
Serves: 6

Grease a 9-inch pie plate.
Form a crust with the shredded potatoes.
Spread meat on top of potatoes.
Combine eggs, seasoning salt and milk.
Pour milk mixture over all.
Bake at 350° for about 40 minutes or until eggs are done.
Spread shredded cheeses on top and return to oven.
Bake until cheeses have melted.
Allow the casserole a few minutes to firm.
Cut in wedges to serve.
Serve with salsa and sour cream if desired

Note: Simply Potatoes can be found in the meat case; they are not frozen.

More Across Colorado

Silverton, 1877.

SILVERTON

"One feels," wrote an early Silverton settler, "as if he is shut off from the rest of the world." A fair assessment: In 1874, when its first buildings appeared, the hamlet lay 125 miles from the nearest post office. Though railroad service commenced in 1882, snowdrifts often blocked the tracks for weeks on end. To compound the isolation, Silverton's climate and topography made farming almost impossible, leaving residents basically dependent on food shipped from elsewhere. But the area's rich mineral deposits - not just gold and silver but also iron, lead, zinc, and copper - assured Silverton's prosperity for many decades. Over time, ironically, remoteness proved to be an asset; it preserved the town's scenery and Victorian character, spurring a robust tourist industry in the mid-twentieth century. One might still feel shut off from the world here, but now that's part of the attraction.

More Across Colorado

Brunch Cheesecake

1 cup whole milk
½ cup melted butter
1½ cups sifted flour
2 cups cottage cheese
2 cups Ricotta, *or* Mascarpone
9 eggs
zest of 2 lemons
unflavored breadcrumbs
sour cream
fruit preserves, *or* sweetened berry purée

Cooking time: 1 hour and 15 minutes
Serves: 6 to 8

Grease 9x13-inch baking pan and sprinkle bottom and sides with breadcrumbs, reserving some for the top.
Combine all ingredients thoroughly and pour into prepared pan. Sprinkle the top with additional breadcrumbs.
Bake at 325° for 1 hour and 15 minutes
Cool for no longer than 10 minutes.
In separate bowls, serve warm with sour cream and with fruit preserves *or* sweetened berry purée.

Note: This brunch dish reminds one of cheese blintzes, but without all of the work of making individual blintzes.

More Across Colorado

Famed photographer William Henry Jackson visited the Virginia Dale Stage Station in 1870 and later made this watercolor from a photo. Though images of the stage station have survived, no definitive photos of Jack Slade are known to exist.

More Across Colorado

VIRGINIA DALE

What a welcome sight Virginia Dale must have been to nineteenth-century travelers. It was one of the largest stagecoach stations on the Overland Trail, offering hot meals and other conveniences to weary passengers - the equivalent, for its day, of an interstate truck stop. Westbound emigrants parked their wagons here, too, restocking their larders and gathering information about the road ahead, while ranchers came from miles around for supplies, conversation, and raucous Saturday-night dances. Founded in 1862, Virginia Dale enjoyed a lively heyday until 1869, when the transcontinental railroad opened to the north. The trail traffic slowed considerably, but the station remained a gathering point for local residents. Used as a community center since the 1940s, the building today stands on private land. It is one of the few original Overland Trail stations still intact.

Jack Slade

Trouble seemed to follow Jack Slade everywhere. He committed his first murder in Illinois at age thirteen, allegedly killed a drinking buddy in Wyoming, and was said to have sliced off a man's ears in eastern Colorado before pumping him full of lead. But he had one legitimate talent - he ran an efficient stagecoach operation - and as long as the line functioned smoothly and the mail arrived on time, Slade's employers could overlook his bullying and boozing. He came to Virginia Dale in 1862 as the Overland Stage Line's division agent; inevitably, though, trouble found him here, too. Suspected of robbing $60,000 from one of his own stages, Slade was fired and sent packing to Montana, where he immediately made new enemies. He died in 1864 at the end of a vigilante's noose.

Chile Relleno Casserole

24 ounces grated Monterey Jack cheese
24 ounces grated cheddar cheese
29-ounce can whole green chiles, rinsed, patted
    dry, split and opened
10 eggs
½ cup flour
½ cup milk
sour cream and salsa, optional

Cooking time: 45 minutes to 1 hour
Serves: 8 to 10

Grease 9x13-inch baking pan. In pan, make 3 layers. First, half the Monterey Jack cheese, half the green chiles (split open and laid out flat), half the cheddar cheese. Second, layer with the remaining half. In large bowl, beat eggs, add flour and milk, and mix well. Pour this mixture evenly over the cheese layers. Bake at 375° for approximately 45 minutes. Check after 30 minutes. Take dish out when top starts to turn golden brown. Allow to set for 15 minutes prior to serving. Cut into squares and serve with sour cream and salsa if desired. Can also serve as a side dish or an appetizer.

Note: Recipe can be halved by using half the ingredients, and baking in 8-inch pan. Adjust baking time.

Crab Quiche

9-inch unbaked pie shell
1 cup shredded Swiss cheese
7½-ounce can crab meat, drained
2 green onions, sliced, including green tops
3 eggs, beaten
1 cup light cream
½ teaspoon salt
½ teaspoon lemon zest
¼ teaspoon mace
¼ cup sliced almonds

Sprinkle cheese evenly over bottom of pie shell. Top with crab meat, then with green onion. Combine remaining ingredients, except almonds. Pour over crab and green onions. Top with almonds. Bake at 325° for 45 minutes or until set.
Let stand a few minutes before cutting into wedges.

Cooking time: 45 minutes
Serves: 6

More Across Colorado

The Hayden Survey.

FERDINAND VANDEVEER HAYDEN
(1829 - 1887)

Between 1859 and 1876, geologist Ferdinand V. Hayden explored privately and for the U.S. Geological and Geographical Survey of the Territories. His expeditions surveyed nearly all of Colorado, producing accurate maps and atlases, fossils for scientific study, and names of mountains (many of which he climbed), rivers, and geological formations. World-famed artist Thomas Moran accompanied him, as did pioneering photographer William H. Jackson, who took the first images of the Mount of the Holy Cross and the Mesa Verde cliff dwellings. While on a surveying expedition in the Yampa River Valley, Hayden's party camped near present-day Hayden, Colorado.

More Across Colorado

Crunchy Chicken Salad Pie

1 tablespoon butter
1½ cups celery, diced in ¼-inch lengths
1 teaspoon grated onion
¼ cup green pepper, chopped
¼ cup red pepper, chopped
2 cups cooked chicken breast, cubed
1 teaspoon salt (or less, to taste)
¼ teaspoon white pepper
½ teaspoon
Accent, optional
1 teaspoon lemon juice
⅓ cup chopped pecans
1½ cups mayonnaise
½ cup grated cheddar cheese
9-inch baked pie shell

Topping:
1 cup finely crushed potato chips

Cooking time: 30 minutes
Serves: 6

Sauté the celery, onion, and peppers in the butter until vegetables are tender-crisp.
Combine all remaining ingredients.
Spoon the mixture into the baked pie shell.
Top with the potato chips.
If pie shell is prepared in advance and chilled, allow it to reach room temperature before baking.
Bake at 350° for 30 minutes, or until heated through.
Let pie rest for 5 to 10 minutes before cutting into wedges and serving.

More Across Colorado

Surveying in the High Country.

More Across Colorado

THE HAYDEN SURVEYS

James Terry Gardiner, a member of Hayden's 1874 Colorado survey expedition, described his experience. "Think of my climbing seven great peaks in nine days. Three of these ascents were over 14,000 feet. For these climbs we rise between three and four in the morning and breakfast by candle light, sitting on the ground in the frosty air with a few coals under our tin plates and cups to keep our food and drink from freezing." Anna E. Dickinson, who met Hayden and his survey party in Colorado in 1873, wrote of the expedition's work. "I looked at him, and all the little party, with ardent curiosity and admiration, braving rain, snow, sleet, hail, hunger, thirst, exposure, bitter nights, snowy climbs, dangers of death for the sake not of a so-called great cause, nor in hot blood, but with patience and unwearied energy for an abstract science."

Crock Pot Fruit

21-ounce can cherry pie filling
15-ounce can pears, drained and cut up
15-ounce can peaches, drained and cut up
½ cup brown sugar, firmly packed
¼ teaspoon nutmeg
½ teaspoon cinnamon

Cooking time: 1 hour
Serves: 6 to 8

Place all ingredients in crock pot and cook on high for 1 hour.
Alternative method:
Place in baking dish and bake at 350° for 30 minutes.

German Pancakes

6 tablespoons butter
6 eggs
1 cup milk
1 cup flour
1 tablespoon sugar
1 teaspoon salt
1 teaspoon vanilla extract
fresh lemon juice, *or* maple syrup
powdered sugar

Cooking time: 15 to 20 minutes
Serves: 4

Preheat oven to 350°.
Place butter in 9x15-inch baking dish and melt in oven. Whisk together eggs, milk, flour, sugar, salt and vanilla.
Pour into baking dish. Bake at 350° for 15 to 20 minutes until nicely browned and puffed, making sure the center is done.
Serve with fresh lemon juice *or* maple syrup, and sprinkle with powdered sugar.

Note: This recipe can also be made using a cast iron skillet instead of a baking dish.

More Across Colorado

MIDDLE PARK SKIING

In Grand County's High Country, skiing is a way of life. Probably the first adults to ski through here for the pure fun of it were two Norwegians, Carl Howelson and Angell Schmidt. In 1911, while skiing through Middle Park, they chanced to come upon the annual winter carnival at Hot Sulphur Springs. Quick to take advantage of an opportunity, the men entertained onlookers with a dazzling demonstration of ski jumping. But large numbers of recreational skiers did not appear until the completion of the Moffat Tunnel in 1928. From then on Middle Park's looming white-topped slopes were only a short train ride away for Denver's snow buffs.

Skiers board the lift at
Berthoud Pass.

More Across Colorado

Mexican Eggs

8 ounces cottage cheese
5 eggs, slightly beaten
1-ounce to 4-ounce can diced green chiles,
    drained
2 cups shredded Monterey Jack cheese
2 tablespoons flour
2 tablespoons butter, melted
½ teaspoon baking powder
sour cream
mild salsa

Cooking time: 45 minutes
Serves: 4 to 6

Generously grease a 9-inch pie plate.
Combine all ingredients. Pour into prepared pie plate.
Bake at 400° for 10 minutes.
Reduce oven temperature to 350° and continue baking 35 minutes more, or until center is set.
Serve with sour cream and mild salsa.

Note: This recipe can be doubled and baked in a 9x13-inch greased baking dish. It will then serve 8 to 10.

More Across Colorado

WINTER PARK

More than just deep snow helped make Winter Park one of the world's great ski resorts. When the Denver, Northwestern & Pacific Railroad - the Moffat Road - topped Rollins Pass in 1905, Denver snow enthusiasts came to ski the slopes from Berthoud Pass to Steamboat Springs. The opening of the Moffat Tunnel in 1928 brought still more ski-lovers, and the tunnel's West Portal quickly became a hub of winter activity. Skiers converted the abandoned shacks of tunnel workers into warming houses and climbed up the steep slopes to schuss down old logging roads. With the help of Denver's manager of parks and improvements, George Cranmer, Winter Park opened in 1940 as part of Denver's world-renowned mountain park system.

The Ski Train arrives in Winter Park.

More Across Colorado

Pumpkin Coffee Cake

Batter:
½ cup butter, softened
¾ cup sugar
1 teaspoon vanilla extract
3 eggs
2 cups flour
1 teaspoon baking powder
1 teaspoon baking soda
1 cup sour cream

Pumpkin mixture:
15-ounce can solid pumpkin
1 egg, slightly beaten
⅓ cup sugar
1 teaspoon pumpkin pie spice

Streusel topping:
1 cup brown sugar
⅓ cup butter
2 teaspoons cinnamon
1 cup chopped nuts

Cooking time: 50 minutes to 1 hour
Serves: 12 to 15

Grease a 9x13-inch baking pan.
Cream together butter, sugar, vanilla and eggs. Beat and set aside.
Whisk together flour, baking powder and baking soda, and add to wet ingredients alternately with sour cream.
Combine pumpkin, egg, sugar and pumpkin pie spice. Set aside.

Streusel topping:
Combine brown sugar, butter, cinnamon and chopped nuts. Set aside.
Spoon half of batter into the prepared pan, spread to corners and edges.
Sprinkle with half of streusel topping.
Spread pumpkin mixture over streusel topping.
Spread remaining batter over pumpkin.
Top with remaining streusel mixture.
Bake at 325° for 50 minutes to 1 hour, or until toothpick inserted in center comes out clean.

Story: This is a favorite with our Colorado Historical Society board, and I promised I would send it to the cookbook. *Mary McInnes Flowers*

More Across Colorado

The Moffat Tunnel.

THE MOFFAT TUNNEL

On April 29, 1922, Colorado voters approved the Moffat Tunnel Bill, and in the next year the U.S. Supreme Court affirmed the legality of using public money to support a private enterprise. Construction began immediately. Crews of hard-rock miners working eight-hour shifts drilled, blasted, mucked, and timbered through the great mountain. Tragically, on July 30, 1926, tons of rock suddenly cut loose from the tunnel's roof: Six men died, more were injured. In all, twenty-eight men died working the tunnel. Opening day came February 26, 1928, when four special trains rumbled through the 6.2-mile bore, the second-longest railroad tunnel in the United States. Steaming 2,400 feet beneath the mountains, trains crossed the Continental Divide in twelve minutes. The scenic but expensive and dangerous five-hour ride over Rollins Pass, often engine-deep in snow, was no more.

More Across Colorado

Sausage Scramble

1½ pounds pork sausage
18 eggs
2 cups milk
1½ teaspoons salt
3 cups (12 ounces) shredded sharp cheddar
garlic-flavored croutons
tomato slices for garnish, optional

Cooking time: 45 to 50 minutes
Serves: 18

Preheat oven to 325°.
Grease a 9x13-inch baking dish.
Cook and stir sausage over medium heat until lightly browned.
Drain and place in prepared baking dish.
Beat eggs, milk and salt together.
Stir in cheese. Pour egg mixture over sausage.
Sprinkle croutons over the top.
Bake uncovered until knife inserted in center comes out clean, 45 to 50 minutes. Let stand 5 minutes before serving.
May be garnished with tomato slices.

Savory Breakfast Casserole

1½ pounds bacon, diced
1 pound sausage
French bread, sliced
1 medium onion, chopped
2 stalks celery, chopped
8 eggs
2 cups milk
1 teaspoon dry mustard
2 cups shredded cheddar cheese

Cooking time: 45 minutes to 1 hour
Serves: 12 to 14

Brown bacon and sausage, and drain the grease.
Grease 13x9-inch baking pan.
Layer French bread on bottom of pan, followed by sausage and bacon, onion and celery.
Combine eggs, milk and mustard. Pour over layers in pan.
Bake at 325° for 45 minutes to 1 hour.
Sprinkle cheese over the top, and return to oven for 5 minutes or until cheese is melted.

More Across Colorado

MARIANO MEDINA

During its brief but colorful life, Mariano Medina's toll bridge and trading post overflowed with high living and tall tales from the proprietor's fur-trapping days. Built on the Big Thompson River in 1858, astride what would become the Overland Trail, Medina's river crossing was one of the first settlements in this region but hardly the last. When the pioneer trail moved three miles east in 1864, so did the settlers, converging around Andrew Douty's flour mill in a town called Old St. Louis. Yet another migration occurred in 1877, when the Colorado Central Railroad pushed through this area. Railroad owner W.A.H. Loveland routed the tracks over the property of his friend David Barnes, who founded his own town there and named it for his benefactor. And so present-day Loveland came into being.

Mariano Medina was one of the few Mexicans who became successful fur trappers in Colorado. He enjoyed a forty-year career as a Mountain Man before establishing his trading post and toll bridge.

More Across Colorado

Swedish Pancakes

4 eggs
2 cups milk
1 teaspoon salt
1 tablespoon sugar
1½ cups flour
6 tablespoons oil
warm syrup, *or* honey
strawberries, optional
whipped cream, optional

Cooking time: 15 minutes
Serves: 4 to 6

Beat eggs until frothy.
Blend in remaining ingredients.
A blender may also be used. Pour paper-thin amount of batter over bottom of very hot greased skillet.
The pancake should be the size of the skillet; they look like crepes.
Turn when lightly brown on bottom.
When done, roll up.

Note: For breakfast, serve with warm syrup, *or* honey. This makes an excellent dessert when filled with strawberries, rolled up and topped with whipped cream.

Story: This is my Grandmother Bergren's recipe. She emigrated from Sweden when she was very young. It is a family favorite, reserved for special Sundays as you can only make a few pancakes at a time (depending on the number of skillets you have going at the same time) – and the cook usually ends up eating after everyone else has finished. *Marianne Galbreath*

More Across Colorado

By the time this photo of Fourth and Cleveland Street was taken c. 1900, Loveland had developed into a substantial town. Today, this neighborhood remains the heart of the downtown business district and is home to government offices, art galleries and restaurants, as well as a number of historic houses and buildings.

LOVELAND

Initially a small agricultural town, Loveland grew into a city after the Great Western Sugar Company built a plant here in 1901. The factory employed hundreds of workers, gave local farmers a profitable market for sugar beets, and recruited waves of immigrants - first Germans from Russia, then Japanese and Hispanos - to work in the beet fields. Great Western dominated the town's economy until 1960, when Hewlett-Packard built a plant here; the high-tech giant soon emerged as the community's largest employer and gave rise to a booming technology sector. Artists have found a welcoming home in Loveland, whose public art program ranks among Colorado's most ambitious. But the city's national claim to fame comes every Valentine's Day, when millions of cards from across the country are routed through here to receive Loveland's distinctive America's Sweetheart postmark.

More Across Colorado

Swiss Quiche

1 cup (4 ounces) shredded Swiss cheese
½ cup cooked broccoli, *or* zucchini, cut in
       small pieces
6 slices bacon, fried and crumbled
4 eggs
2 cups whipping cream
¾ teaspoon salt
¼ teaspoon sugar
sprinkle onion salt
9-inch unbaked pie shell

Cooking time: 45 minutes to 1 hour
Serves: 6 to 8

Place Swiss cheese, broccoli *or* zucchini, and crumbled bacon in pie shell.
Combine eggs and whipping cream and beat lightly.
Mix in the dry ingredients and pour into pie shell.
Bake at 425° for 15 minutes.
Turn oven down to 325°.
Continue cooking for 30 to 45 minutes.
Let stand for 5 minutes to set.

Waffles

2 cups Bisquick
1 egg, beaten
2 tablespoons corn oil – ***do not substitute***
1 cup club soda

Cooking time: 15 minutes
Serves: 4

Combine all ingredients.
Cook in medium-hot waffle iron until golden brown, approximately 5 minutes.
Best when served immediately; can be placed in single layer on cookie sheet in warm oven until ready to serve.

Note: These waffles are nice and crisp, yet very tender.

More Across Colorado

Photographed in the mid-1880s, the entire population of Walden consisted of Doc Squires (a veterinarian) and the Shippery, Greene, and Rathburn families. Ike Greene (standing third from left) built the town's first house.

WALDEN

The proprietor of an early Walden saloon built the doors high and wide enough to let cowboys ride in without ever dismounting. He obviously knew his market: Cattle ranchers, who came to Walden from miles around for supplies and services. Founded in 1889 by refugees from the Teller City mining bust, it was the only incorporated town in North Park and a vital link to the world beyond the basin. Walden became the Jackson County seat in 1909 and welcomed a railroad two years later to serve the nearby coal mine. The timber industry thrived, too: The 1990 White House Christmas Tree was cut just a few miles from here. But at its core Walden has always been a cow town, in the best sense of the phrase - an authentic ranching community, steeped in the lore of the West.

More Across Colorado

Apple Fritters

cooking oil
1 cup flour
½ teaspoon salt
1½ teaspoons baking powder
1 tablespoon sugar
1 egg, beaten
1 cup sliced tart apples
½ cup milk
1 tablespoon butter, melted
powdered sugar and cinnamon

Cooking time: 3 to 4 minutes
Serves: 6

Heat oil in deep fryer according to directions.
Combine remaining ingredients.
Drop by heaping tablespoons into fryer.
Turn when golden brown.
Cook 3 to 4 minutes, until golden brown.
Sprinkle with powdered sugar and cinnamon.
Serve warm.

Maureen Scanlon
Healy House Museum
Leadville, Colorado

More Across Colorado

"If I succeed in putting Denver on a through transcontinental line, I will then think I have done something for my state." David H. Moffat.

THE MOFFAT ROAD

David Moffat began life as a poor boy in New York. In the 1860s he moved to the rough mining camp of Denver and eventually made a fortune in banks, mines, and railroads. In 1903 he embarked on his most ambitious project, building the Denver, Northwestern & Pacific Railroad, known to all simply as the Moffat Road. He intended for his line to cross the central Rockies from Denver to the west. But construction drained Moffat's fortunes, and when he died in 1911 his dream was unfulfilled. Others picked up where Moffat left off. In 1928 the Moffat Tunnel was completed, opening up northwestern Colorado, but the rails ended in Craig. Not until 1934, when the Denver & Rio Grande Railroad bought out Moffat's road and the Dotsero Cutoff allowed their tracks to link, was his dream of placing Denver squarely on a transcontinental line realized.

More Across Colorado

Apple Pudding

1 egg, beaten
¾ cup sugar
1 teaspoon baking powder
2 tablespoons flour
pinch of salt
1 teaspoon vanilla extract
1 cup chopped nut meats
1 large apple, chopped

Cooking time: 45 minutes
Serves: 6

Add sugar to beaten egg, and beat again.
Sift baking powder, flour and salt together.
Add to egg and sugar, and beat again.
Add vanilla, nuts and apple, and beat again.
Grease an 8-inch square baking pan.
Pour batter into pan.
Bake at 350° for 45 minutes.

Story: This is Zelmer (Mrs. George) Omohundro's recipe. She was my mother and president of the Park Hill Methodist Church's Ladies Aid. They started the Wednesday Night Suppers in the gym to pay off the church building. They used Mother's recipes, and she would go to the Farmer's Market in downtown Denver and buy that week's ingredients. The ladies would come to the church and cook; Mother was always in the kitchen. After school on Wednesdays I'd go over with some of the girls and we'd set up the tables and serve the coffee. Jack and Ruth Winton always stood at the door and collected the quarter admission. About 50 people would come eat, cafeteria style. When my brother, Edward Lee, was recuperating from an eye infection, he and Mother sat side by side and worked up the recipes into a cookbook. I have that original cookbook.
As told to Paulette Whitcomb by Jean Omohundro McLaughlin, now 89 years young.

More Across Colorado

ARGO'S SQUIRRELS

Perhaps no section of the Denver, Northwestern & Pacific Railroad offered as great a challenge as Gore Canyon: Six miles long and impossibly narrow, with sheer granite walls rising 3,000 feet. To survey the canyon required men with steel nerve and great physical stamina. Mostly immigrants, they came to be known as Argo's Squirrels after J. J. Argo, the man in charge. Dangling from ropes dropped over the cliffs, they drove steel pegs into the granite. Logs tied down with steel cables were then floated downriver, hoisted up the walls, and secured to the pegs. From these footbridges swinging high above the river, the Squirrels conducted the survey. No life was lost, but the Squirrels themselves would tolerate no man among them who seemed to lose his nerve.

Going to work Gore Canon July '05.

At work on the Moffat Road in Gore Canyon, 1905.

More Across Colorado

Bread Pudding with Caramel Sauce

Pudding:
1 day-old loaf French bread, in ½-inch-thick slices
3 eggs
3 cups milk, *or* half-and-half
½ cup sugar
1 teaspoon vanilla
1 teaspoon cinnamon
1 teaspoon nutmeg
½ teaspoon salt, optional
optional additions: walnuts, raisins, blueberries, quartered dried apricots

Topping:
¾ pound butter, cut into small pieces
1 cup flour
½ cup sugar
½ cup brown sugar

Caramel sauce:
2 cups sugar
2 cups heavy cream

Cooking time: 1 hour to 1¼ hours
Serves: 8

Line a spring form pan with buttered parchment paper. Soak bread briefly in mixture of next 7 ingredients. Layer bread mixture in pan. This is the time to sprinkle in any optional ingredients.

Topping:
Cut together all topping ingredients until mixture looks like coarse cornmeal and sprinkle over bread mixture. Prepare a water bath, and place spring form pan inside a larger pan. Add hot water to outside pan until water reaches halfway up sides of inside pan. Bake at 350° for 1 to 1¼ hours, or until golden brown.

Caramel sauce:
While pudding bakes, stir sugar and 1½ cups of cream in a saucepan over medium heat until sugar dissolves. Turn up heat and continue to cook at a boil, swirling mixture by the pot handle, until mixture turns golden brown. Be very careful, as mixture will bubble up and be very hot. Watch carefully to avoid burning the mixture. It will thicken more as it cools. Remove from heat, fold in the remaining cream and stir. Again, be careful, as mixture will bubble up. Mix until sauce is smooth. Remove pan from water bath and let cool. Invert cooled pudding onto a plate; remove parchment paper. Then invert again onto a serving platter so topping is on top. Serve with caramel sauce. Leftover sauce can be used on ice cream.
Carol Toth, Manager, Highland's Garden Café, Denver, Colorado

More Across Colorado

Old Main at Colorado State University burned on May 9, 1970.

DEMOCRACY'S COLLEGE

Determined to establish an agricultural school, Fort Collins boosters planted a twenty-acre demonstration plot in 1874. They patiently sought support in the state legislature, and in September 1879 the Colorado Agricultural College opened its doors. The institution's primary mission was to develop and teach scientific methods for farming in Colorado's high, dry environment. But the school also pursued a new, more public-spirited approach to education. Dubbed Democracy's College, it catered to those denied access to traditional universities: women, rural populations, and the working class. With its progressive outlook, the agricultural school helped produce the first crop of twentieth-century Coloradans. Later renamed the Colorado State College of Agricultural and Mechanical Arts, and eventually Colorado State University, the institution now grants undergraduate and graduate degrees in hundreds of academic disciplines.

More Across Colorado

Breakfast Cookies

1 cup sugar, *or* ½ cup honey
2 ripe bananas
1 egg
¾ cup softened butter
1½ cups flour, *or* ½ white and ½ whole wheat
½ teaspoon baking soda
¼ teaspoon *each* salt, nutmeg and cinnamon
1¾ cups oatmeal (Quick, *or* Old Fashioned)
6 ounces chocolate chips, *or* butterscotch chips
½ cup *each* raisins *or* Craisins, dried fruit,
       coconut, nut meats, chopped dates

Cream together first 4 ingredients.
Stir in dry ingredients.
Add in any or all of the fruits, chips and nuts.
Combine ingredients.
Drop by rounded tablespoons on ungreased cookie sheet.
Bake at 350° for about 15 minutes, or until golden brown.

Cooking time: about 15 minutes

Brownies

2 cups sugar
4 eggs
10 tablespoons milk
1 cup butter, melted
8 tablespoons cocoa
dash of salt
2 cups flour
½ cup powdered sugar for topping

Cooking time: 15 to 20 minutes
Yield: 20

Mix sugar, eggs, milk and butter until creamy.
Add cocoa, salt and flour.
Pour into a greased 9x13-inch baking pan.
Bake at 350° for 15 to 20 minutes.
When brownies are cooled, sprinkle with powdered sugar, cut into squares and serve.

More Across Colorado

Motorists atop Berthoud Pass.

More Across Colorado

BERTHOUD PASS

As early as the 1870s, wagons carried tourists, supplies, and the U.S. mail over Berthoud Pass. By 1920, automobiles braved its unimproved roads, yet it was only with the building of U.S. Highway 40 that Berthoud Pass became part of a major transcontinental route. From the days of the Gold Rush, Coloradans had looked for a way to cross the Rockies. In 1861, Mountain Man Jim Bridger came down from Wyoming to help civil engineer Edward Louis Berthoud survey a stage road west of Denver. Berthoud found his pass and built a rough road through Middle Park and across the plateau country and Wasatch Mountains to Provo, Utah. Then came talk of a transcontinental railroad. If Colorado were to be on the Union Pacific's main route, the railroad's engineers would have to be convinced of the feasibility of building a line over Berthoud Pass. They were not; the Union Pacific passed through Wyoming instead. Still, Middle Park residents remained optimistic, and by the 1870s wagons rolled over Berthoud Pass to stops along the Fraser River and on to the spas at Hot Sulphur Springs. But in the poignant words of Grand County historian Robert C. Black III, "The new country [opened by Berthoud Pass] was what Middle Park had always been: an island, engulfed by mountains, whose power to [isolate] had been lessened only a little."

Butter Caramels

3 cups white sugar
1⅔ cups white corn syrup
1 cup butter – *do not substitute*
2 cups coffee cream
walnuts, optional

Cooking time: 20 to 40 minutes
Yield: 81 pieces

In a heavy pan, combine all the ingredients, except for 1 cup of the cream. Cook *very slowly*. When it comes to a boil, add the remaining 1 cup of cream. Cook until firm ball stage (232°), or until a firm ball is formed when a small amount is dropped in ice-cold water. Process takes 20 to 40 minutes.
Add finely chopped walnuts, if desired. Pour into a buttered 9-inch square pan.
Cool, then cut into squares and wrap in wax paper or plastic wrap.

Note: They keep for months.

Story: In the 1930s, Mrs. Russell Stover made candies in her kitchen during the Depression. She lived in a bungalow in South Denver and called her candies Mrs. Stover's Bungalow Candies. She was a patient of my father's, and I spent hours sitting in the car waiting for my father to make a house call. My mother sent her a gift of her homemade caramels, and Mrs. Stover offered her $40 (a princely sum, then) for the recipe. My mother refused and carefully guarded this recipe for years, as she made huge batches at Christmas. Trust me – these are fabulous. *Eleanor Hixon*

More Across Colorado

Routt County coal miners.

KING COAL

Coal! The sound of it doesn't evoke the romance of silver and gold, but in the Yampa River Valley coal is the undisputed king of minerals. Coal by the billions of tons lies in seams at or just beneath the ground's surface, a fact long ago reported by explorers and government surveyors. But in this remote country far from coal markets, large-scale mining awaited the coming of a railroad. That happened in 1908 with the Denver, Northwest & Pacific Railway - the famed Moffat Road - and northwestern Colorado has never been the same. Today, out of Colorado's eight major coal regions, thirteen mines in Routt and Moffat counties account for over half of the state's total coal production. King Coal's throne stands in the Yampa River Valley.

More Across Colorado

Cappuccino Mousse Trifle

1 pound frozen prepared pound cake
2½ cups cold milk
⅓ cup instant coffee granules
2 3.4-ounce packages vanilla instant pudding
       and pie filling
2 8-ounce containers frozen whipped topping,
       thawed
¼ teaspoon cinnamon
1-ounce square semi-sweet baking chocolate

Serves: 10

Cut pound cake into 1-inch cubes; set aside.
Combine milk and instant coffee granules using whisk.
Allow to dissolve for 5 minutes.
Set aside 1 cup of milk mixture.
Add pudding mix to remaining milk mixture in bowl; whisk until mixture begins to thicken.
Gently fold in one container of whipped topping.

To assemble trifle:
Place one-third of cake cubes into bottom of bowl.
Pour one-third of reserved milk mixture evenly over cake cubes.
Top with one-third of pudding mixture, pressing lightly.
Grate one-fourth of chocolate over pudding mixture.
Repeat layers twice more, reserving remaining grated chocolate for garnish.
Spread whipped topping over entire top of trifle, creating a smooth surface.
Sprinkle with cinnamon and remaining grated chocolate.
Chill thoroughly before serving.

More Across Colorado

Rotary plow at Rollins Pass.

ROLLINS PASS

Rollins Pass defined the Moffat Road - David Moffat's Denver, Northwestern & Pacific Railway, which promised to place Denver on a direct coast-to-coast railroad line. Rail buffs and travelers in general thrilled to pictures of steaming Mallet engines rigged with rotary snowplows mightily working to the 11,660-foot summit of Rollins Pass. It was the stuff of legend, but Rollins Pass bankrupted the railroad - and David Moffat. For the Moffat Road to prove its promise, some other way would have to be found to get over or under the Colorado Rockies.

More Across Colorado

Caramel Apple Crostata

dough for 9-inch pie crust, unbaked
¼ cup butter
½ cup sugar
3 to 4 Fiji apples – *or* your favorite apple –
    peeled and sliced
½ to ¾ teaspoon cinnamon
½ teaspoon nutmeg
1 tablespoon cornstarch
1 tablespoon water
2 tablespoons heavy cream
1 jar hot caramel sauce

Cooking time: 45 minutes
Serves: 6 to 8

In a large skillet, melt the butter, add the sugar, and cook until light brown – about 2 minutes.
Add the apples and cook until they are just barely soft.
Add the spices, mixing well.
Dissolve the cornstarch in the water and add to the apple mixture, mixing well.
Cook 1 minute.
Remove from heat and cool.
Roll out dough to a 10-inch circle and place on a parchment-lined cookie sheet.
Mound the filling in the center.
Bring edges up over the filling, folding as needed, leaving a 3-inch to 4-inch opening in the center.
Brush with the heavy cream.
Bake at 350° for 45 minutes until crust is crisp and browned.
Allow to cool slightly before serving.
Cut in wedges.
Serve warm with hot caramel sauce.

More Across Colorado

The Utes are a confederation of seven bands—Moache, Capote, Weeminuche, Tabeguache, Grand River, Yampa, and Uintah. Today, the Moache and Capote comprise the Southern Utes; the Weeminuche, the Ute Mountain Utes; and the other four bands, the Northern Utes.

More Across Colorado

HOOSIER PASS

For many centuries, Hoosier Pass served as a link between two important Ute hunting grounds: South Park and Middle Park, the heart of the tribe's mountain domain. By the 1400s or 1500s these hunter-gatherers occupied territory from Utah's desert to the Front Range of present-day Colorado. Their mastery of the horse, introduced by the Spaniards in the 1600s, and their superior topographical knowledge made the Utes powerful warriors, and they routinely dispatched the other tribes who challenged them for control of South Park. Although early non-Indian visitors generally went unchallenged, permanent settlers were not welcome. But in the late nineteenth century, the tide of pioneers finally forced the Utes out of their mountain strongholds. By the 1880s, they had been confined to reservations in Colorado and Utah.

Cheese Cake

This recipe calls for day-ahead preparation. *

Crust:
16 to 20 graham crackers, crushed
4 tablespoons butter, melted
2 tablespoons sugar

Filling:
2 eggs
1 pound dry, small-curd cottage cheese, *or*
      creamy style for creamier texture
½ cup sugar
½ teaspoon vanilla

Topping:
12 ounces sour cream
2 tablespoons sugar
½ teaspoon vanilla

Cooking time: 25 minutes
Serves: 8 to 10

Crust:
Combine all ingredients.
Reserve some of crust mixture for the top.
Press into the bottom and up the sides of a 9-inch spring form pan.
Set aside.

Filling:
Combine all ingredients and spoon over crust.
If you prefer a smoother texture, purée the cottage cheese in a blender or food processor before mixing with other ingredients.

Bake at 375° for 20 minutes.
Cool.

Topping:
Combine all topping ingredients.
Spread on top of cheese cake.
Sprinkle reserved crust crumbs on top.
Bake at 475° for 5 minutes.

* *Refrigerate overnight.*

More Across Colorado

WOODLAND PARK

A Colorado Midland wildflower excursion, c. 1900.

Platted in 1873, the little colony at Manitou Park (precursor to Woodland Park) was a strange hybrid indeed: half logging camp, half summer resort. But the well-heeled guests at the two-story lodge learned to live with the local lumberjacks (and vice versa), and this marriage of working and leisure class proved a prosperous one. Both halves benefited from the 1887 arrival of the Colorado Midland Railroad, which delivered visitors and shipped out timber at vastly accelerated rates. Renamed Woodland Park in 1891, it ranked among Colorado's most fashionable vacation spots until after World War I, when the railroad discontinued passenger service, thus thinning the tourist traffic. However, the emergence of automobile travel helped to offset these losses. As highway improvements eased the commute into Colorado Springs, Woodland Park evolved into a popular year-round residential community.

Chocolate Waffle Cookies

1 cup margarine
1½ cups sugar
8 eggs
2 teaspoons vanilla extract
½ cup cocoa powder
2 cups flour
½ cup chopped black walnuts, optional

Icing:
4 cups powdered sugar
⅓ cup cocoa powder
¼ cup brewed coffee – just enough to make
    icing smooth but not stiff

Cooking time: 1 hour
Yield: 4 dozen

Cream margarine and sugar in large mixing bowl.
Add eggs and mix well.
Add vanilla and cocoa, mixing well.
Add flour gradually, mixing well.
Add nuts, if desired.
Grease the waffle iron and heat to medium.
Drop by teaspoonfuls on hot waffle iron.
Bake about 2 minutes or until done.
Be careful: They burn fast.
Try one cookie first on the waffle iron to see if more flour is needed.
Frost the cookies while warm using the icing recipe. They are also good with no icing.

Story: My nephew, Mike Peterson, was a State Representative, and he asked me to make 50 of these cookies for his birthday for the House of Representatives. The senators heard about it and came over. Everyone wanted the recipe. The next year we made over 200. My daughter helped this time by frosting them, but it still took a long time. *Sandra Smith*

More Across Colorado

One of Colorado's first ski clubs, the Snow Shoe Brigade, near Gunnison, c. 1880. The single pole was used for balance and braking.

EARLY RECREATIONAL SKIING

Though Colorado's first ski clubs formed as early as the nineteenth century, the activity hardly qualified as recreation. Practitioners had to hoof it up the slope, then find their way down without the aid of signs, cleared trails, safety markers, or groomed snow. Very few caught the bug. That began to change in the 1910s, when winter festivals popularized all manner of cold-weather amusements. The 1932 Winter Olympics at Lake Placid, New York, further broadened interest in the sport, and newly improved mountain highways paved the way for a number of Colorado resort openings. These prewar locales (including Berthoud Pass, Loveland, Monarch, and Winter Park) offered a hardy, adventurous brand of skiing with few luxuries. But enough people discovered the joys of schussing to give rise to a new Colorado industry.

More Across Colorado

Choco-Mint Freeze

1¼ cups finely crushed vanilla wafers (about 28 wafers)
4 tablespoons butter, melted
1 quart peppermint ice cream, softened
2 squares (2 ounces) unsweetened chocolate
½ cup butter
3 well-beaten egg yolks
1½ cups sifted powdered sugar
½ cup chopped pecans
1 teaspoon vanilla extract
3 egg whites

Serves: 8

Toss together the wafer crumbs and melted butter.
Reserve one-quarter of this crumb mixture.
Press the remaining mixture into a 9x9x2-inch baking pan.
Spread with the softened ice cream.
Freeze.
Melt butter and chocolate over low heat.
Gradually stir into egg yolks along with the powdered sugar, nuts and vanilla.
Cool thoroughly.
Beat egg whites until stiff peaks form.
Beat chocolate mixture until smooth; fold in egg whites.
Spread chocolate mixture over frozen ice cream.
Top with reserved crumb mixture.
Return to freezer.

More Across Colorado

The ski lift completely changed the face of the sport by allowing skiers to take many more runs with much less work. Today, high-speed, multi-passenger chairs are a far cry from Colorado's first rope tow installed at Berthoud Pass in 1937.

More Across Colorado

SKIING TECHNOLOGY

Colorado's first ski lift, a surface-level rope tow unveiled at Berthoud Pass Ski Area in 1937, guaranteed rapid, effortless ascent for skiers - and skiing's popularity. Subsequent technologies (T-bars, chairlifts, gondolas) made the ride uphill even more rapid and convenient, while innovations such as slope groomers (invented in 1957) and snowmaking machines (popularized in the 1980s) ensured uniformly good conditions. They also, however, generated some grumbling about the sport's increasing tameness. Equipment makers responded with faster, lighter skis, and the high-flying snowboard provided new thrills; by the new millennium, roughly one-fourth of Colorado resort visitors were snowboarding. Others turned to rugged variants such as backcountry skiing, snowshoeing, and telemark skiing, which harkened back to the sport's beginnings. No lifts, no machines - just mountains and snow, and skiers propelled by their lungs and their muscles.

Cinnamon Apple Cake

cooking spray
1¾ cups sugar
¾ cup (6 ounces) block-style, fat-free cream
    cheese, softened
½ cup butter, *or* stick margarine, softened
1 teaspoon vanilla extract
2 large eggs
1½ cups flour
1½ teaspoons baking powder
¼ teaspoon salt
2 teaspoons ground cinnamon
3 cups peeled and chopped Rome apples (about
    2 large apples)

Cooking time: 1 hour and 15 minutes
Serves: 12

Preheat oven to 350°.

Spray an 8-inch spring form pan with cooking spray.

Beat 1½ cups of the sugar with the cream cheese, butter *or* margarine, and vanilla with electric mixer at medium speed until well blended – about 4 minutes.

Add eggs, one at a time, beating well after each addition; set aside.

Combine the flour, baking powder and salt; stir with a wire whisk to blend.

Add flour mixture to creamed mixture, and beat on low speed until blended.

Combine the remaining sugar and the cinnamon.

In a bowl, combine 2 tablespoons of the cinnamon mixture with the apples.

Stir apple mixture into batter.

Pour batter into prepared pan and sprinkle with remaining cinnamon mixture.

Bake at 350° for 1 hour and 15 minutes, or until cake pulls away from the sides of pan.

Cool cake completely on wire rack.

Note: The cream cheese in the batter gives this cake lots of moisture. Because it's so tender, use a serrated knife for cutting.

More Across Colorado

GUNNISON

Gunnison's Tomichi Avenue and Pine Street.

The town of Gunnison dates to 1874, when Sylvester Richardson built a cluster of cabins on the Gunnison River. His settlement, however, languished until the 1879-1880 Silver Rush. The cry, "Ho for the Gunnison!" transformed a forgotten shantytown into a wide-awake camp of over 2,000 residents. By the summer of 1881, Gunnison was the major supply town for all the surrounding mining camps, as the countryside was rich in deposits of gold, silver, coal, marble, iron, and sandstone. The Denver & Rio Grande Railroad arrived in 1881, and Gunnison's future seemed assured. But the Panic of 1893 destroyed the mineral boom, and Gunnison fell on hard times, not to recover until the recent boom of "white gold" - skiing.

More Across Colorado

Coffee Mousse in Meringue Shells

Meringues:
3 egg whites
1 teaspoon vanilla extract
¼ teaspoon cream of tartar
1 cup sugar

Coffee mousse:
2 tablespoons instant coffee, *or* ⅓ cup espresso
      (in which case, omit boiling water)
⅓ cup boiling water
1 envelope unflavored gelatin
3 egg yolks
½ cup powdered sugar
3 egg whites
2 cups whipping cream

Topping:
½ cup finely chopped pecans, *or* walnuts

Cooking time: 3 to 4 hours
Serves: 6 to 12

Meringues:
Place room-temperature egg whites in mixing bowl.
Add vanilla and cream of tartar.
Beat until egg whites reach soft peaks.
Begin adding sugar, 2 to 3 tablespoons at a time.
Whites are ready when all of the sugar has been incorporated and the whites form stiff peaks and are glossy.
Cover a cookie sheet with brown or parchment paper.
Form either 6 large or 12 smaller shells; using a spoon, make a depression in the center of each.
Bake at 200° for 3 to 4 hours, or until the meringues have dried out, as it were.

Coffee mousse:
Add coffee to boiling water and dissolve, *or* use espresso.
Cool slightly.
Add gelatin to coffee and dissolve.
Beat egg yolks and powdered sugar until pale yellow and thick.
Beat egg whites until soft peaks form.
Whip the cream.
Fold all ingredients together. Fill shells and top with nuts.

See **Mousse au Chocolat** for an alternative meringue filling.

More Across Colorado

Before airplanes were used to spot blazes, Pike National Forest housed seventeen fire lookouts. Today, Devil's Head Tower remains the only fully staffed fire lookout in Colorado. Originally, the tower was reached first by a tree ladder, then a series of 30-foot poles with nailed lateral slats. Now visitors use a staircase and railing. Nearby are a public campground and picnic area.

More Across Colorado

TIMBER

Woodland Park in the 1870s was ideally positioned to develop a successful logging industry. In addition to an abundant supply of raw timber, it enjoyed easy access to the wide, well-kept Ute Pass wagon road; to nearby markets in rapidly growing Denver and Colorado Springs, whose hunger for lumber never seemed to abate; and, after 1887, to railroad service on the Colorado Midland, whose superior freight capacity spurred giant leaps in production. The 1890 gold rush at nearby Cripple Creek generated massive new demand for building materials, and by century's end Woodland Park was shipping 12 million board-feet per year. That was the industry's peak. Demand soon depleted the resource, signaling the end of unfettered cutting. Today the community bears few traces of its timber-town origins.

Pike National Forest

By 1890, after twenty-plus years of intensive logging, the forests near Woodland Park had been stripped of marketable timber. Lest they vanish altogether, President Benjamin Harrison included the remaining stands in three timber preserves in the 1890s; in 1905 they were combined into the 1.1-million-acre Pike National Forest. Federal oversight of logging, grazing, and mining drew angry resistance at first; the outcry subsided as the benefits of resource management - including fire-fighting, soil conservation, and watershed protection - became apparent. After World War II, outdoor enthusiasts flocked to the forest in ever-increasing numbers, to the point that recreation has replaced logging as the preserve's primary use. Over the last half of the twentieth century, the Pike consistently ranked among the country's ten most heavily visited national forests.

Creamy Chocolate Fudge

½ cup butter
12-ounce can evaporated milk
4 cups sugar
10-ounce Hershey Bar without nuts
13-ounce jar marshmallow cream
4 cups semi-sweet chocolate chips
1 cup chopped nuts, optional

Cooking time: 15 minutes
Yield: 3 to 4 dozen 1-inch squares

Place butter, evaporated milk and sugar in large pan.
Bring to a full boil and boil for 5 minutes, stirring frequently.
Remove from heat.
Stir in remaining ingredients.
Pour into 10x15-inch buttered jelly-roll pan to cool.
Cut into 1-inch squares.

Famous Oatmeal Cookies

¾ cup shortening (soft)
1 cup firmly packed brown sugar
½ cup granulated sugar
1 egg
¼ cup water
1 teaspoon vanilla extract
1 cup sifted flour
1 teaspoon salt
½ teaspoon baking soda
3 cups oats, uncooked
optional additions: chopped nuts, raisins,
        chocolate chips or coconut

Preheat to 350°, or moderate heat.
Beat together shortening, sugars, egg, water and vanilla extract until creamy.
Sift together flour, salt and soda. Add to creamed mixture and blend well. Stir in oats.
Drop by teaspoonful onto greased cookie sheets.
Bake at 350° for 12 to 15 minutes.

Cooking time: 12 to 15 minutes
Yield: 5 dozen cookies

More Across Colorado

Hoosier Pass summit, about 1920.

THE CONTINENTAL DIVIDE

Hoosier Pass lies on the Continental Divide, the lofty meandering spine of mountains that separates the Atlantic and Pacific watersheds. Nineteenth-century pioneers dreaded the barrier, particularly its high, difficult Colorado stretches; for that reason many westbound emigrants and early railroad builders avoided the region altogether, seeking lower and easier crossings in Wyoming or New Mexico. Railroads and highways eventually eased the passage, but the Divide retained a definite mystique, even when water started flowing under and through it. During the twentieth century, almost forty pipeline, tunnel, and ditch projects breached the Divide, transferring hundreds of billions of gallons a year from the Western Slope to the more heavily populated Front Range. Impermeable no longer, the Divide evolved from a physical boundary into a political one - the front line in the West's water wars.

More Across Colorado

French Lemon Pie

This recipe may require day-ahead preparation. *

Crust:
2½ cups graham cracker crumbs
½ cup butter, melted
4 tablespoons sugar

Filling:
1 large can evaporated milk
2 3-ounce packages lemon gelatin
½ cup hot water
½ cup sugar
2 teaspoons lemon zest
¼ cup lemon juice (juice of 2 lemons)

Yield: 2 pies

Crust:
With a fork, mix graham cracker crumbs, butter and sugar.
Reserve 2 tablespoons for topping.
Divide remaining crust mixture between two 9-inch pie plates.
Press crumbs onto bottom and up the sides of the pie plates.
Refrigerate.

Filling:
Pour evaporated milk into ice tray and chill in freezer until crystals form.
Combine gelatin, water, sugar and 2 tablespoons of the lemon juice.
Stir until gelatin is dissolved.
Chill until thick.
Whip the evaporated milk with remaining 2 tablespoons of the lemon juice until thick.
Add the gelatin mixture and lemon zest to the milk mixture and whip until fluffy.
Pour into chilled crusts. Top with sprinkles of the reserved graham cracker mixture.
* *Refrigerate 6 hours.*

Serve chilled.

More Across Colorado

FATHER JOHN DYER

The Rev. John Dyer must have crossed Hoosier Pass a thousand times - almost always on foot, and often in the dead of winter. His sprawling Methodist ministry, launched in 1861, took him from Breckenridge to Fairplay, Leadville, and every rough mining camp in between. To expedite his alpine amblings, Father Dyer strapped on skis (one of the first Coloradans to do so), bringing him great renown as the "Snowshoe Itinerant" (as skis were then called); he also carried the winter mail to supplement his meager income. This curious figure must have puzzled and amazed the coarse men of the frontier, but he was as tough as they were, letting neither high mountains nor low morals deter him. Unlike most of them, he had come to stay - and his work helped build lasting communities.

John Dyer and his children, late 1840s. A Methodist minister from Wisconsin, Dyer first came to Colorado in 1861 intending to return to the Midwest. When he learned that the region lacked religious instruction, he decided to stay, and he remained in Colorado until his death in 1901. A memorial to Dyer is located near the summit of Mosquito Pass.

More Across Colorado

Fresh Peach Pie

9-inch graham-cracker, *or* shortbread crust
2 cups water
3-ounce package sugar-free peach gelatin
8-ounce package sugar-free, cook-and-serve,
      vanilla pudding mix
6 fresh peaches

Cooking time: 6 minutes
Serves: 6

Pour water in shallow pan.
Add gelatin and pudding; blend.
Boil for 6 minutes, stirring while it boils.
Cool in refrigerator until partially set (approximately 1 hour).
Meanwhile, peel and cut the peaches into bite-size pieces.
Stir peaches into pudding-gelatin mixture.
Spoon into crust and chill for 2 to 3 hours.

German Chocolate Cookies

½ cup granulated sugar
1¾ sticks butter
3 eggs
¼ teaspoon salt
scant ½ teaspoon baking soda
½ cup flour
3½ cups Quick oatmeal
1 cup chocolate chips
¾ cup walnuts, chopped
1 cup coconut flakes

Cooking time: 10 to 12 minutes
Yield: 30 cookies

Cream together sugar and butter.
Add eggs and blend.
Add salt, baking soda and flour to mixture.
Add oatmeal.
Blend well.
Stir in chocolate chips, nuts and coconut.
Drop by tablespoonful onto non-stick cookie sheet.
Bake at 325° for 10 to 12 minutes.

More Across Colorado

Pikes Peak from Manitou Park Station.

RESORT TOWNS

In addition to fueling Woodland Park's growth, the Colorado Midland Railroad spawned a number of new resort communities between that city and Colorado Springs. Cascade, Chipita Park, and Green Mountain Falls, all built right beside the tracks in the late 1880s, boasted ornate hotels and a range of healthful diversions for a mostly urban clientele. Visitors fanned into the neighboring countryside to hike, fish, swim, ride horseback, pick wildflowers, or simply enjoy the views. Those inclined toward thrills might take a carriage ride up the treacherous Pikes Peak Toll Road, while more sedentary guests could opt for rest and fresh air at a guest ranch. Although hurt by the railroad's decision to end passenger service in 1922, these towns retooled for the era of automobile travel, with motels, bed-and-breakfasts, and campgrounds for a new brand of vacationer.

More Across Colorado

Ice Cream Torte

This recipe may require day-ahead preparation. *

Crust:
1½ cups shortbread cookie crumbs
¼ cup packed light brown sugar
¼ teaspoon ground nutmeg
¼ cup butter, melted

Filling:
1 quart butter pecan ice cream
¾ cup Irish Creme liqueur
12-ounce jar caramel ice cream topping
1 cup coarsely chopped pecans, toasted
1 quart chocolate ice cream
12-ounce jar fudge ice cream topping

Serves: 16

Crust:
Lightly butter sides of 10-inch spring form pan; line sides with strips of waxed paper; butter bottom and paper-lined sides of pan. In small bowl, mix shortbread crumbs, sugar and nutmeg. Stir in melted butter. Pat evenly on bottom of pan; refrigerate.

Filling, first layer:
Spoon slightly softened butter pecan ice cream into medium-size bowl and swirl in ½ cup of liqueur. ***Do not overmix.*** Pack into chilled crust. Pour caramel topping into small bowl and stir in 2 tablespoons of liqueur. Spoon over butter pecan layer; sprinkle with ¾ cup pecans. Freeze 1 hour.

Filling, second layer:
Spread slightly softened chocolate ice cream on top of frozen first layer. Freeze at least 1 hour. Pour fudge topping into small bowl and stir in remaining 2 tablespoons of liqueur; spoon over chocolate ice cream.

* *Cover with foil and freeze until firm, about 6 hours **or** overnight.*

To serve, remove sides of pan; peel off waxed paper. Place bottom of pan on a serving plate. Garnish torte top with remaining ¼ cup of pecans. Let torte stand 10 minutes before slicing.

More Across Colorado

During a group outing, some tourists pose on a large petrified tree stump.

FLORISSANT FOSSIL BEDS

Though bereft of gold and silver, the ground around Florissant yielded something just as precious: A fossil record stretching back more than 35 million years. Prehistoric peoples and later the Utes probably knew about this rich deposit of petrified insects and plants, which explorers and settlers rediscovered in the late 1860s. A local attraction in the 1870s, the fossil beds drew crowds of curious tourists by the late 1880s via Colorado Midland special excursion trains. Although the railroad discontinued passenger service after World War I and thus briefly thinned the crowds, private owners revived the attraction as a popular guest ranch and resort. But when a real estate developer proposed to build over a large portion of the valley in the mid-1960s, concerned scientists and some local residents appealed for federal protection; this came in 1969 with the creation of Florissant Fossil Beds National Monument. Still renowned for its wealth of specimens, this paleontological plenitude draws researchers from around the world.

More Across Colorado

Kentucky Bourbon Balls

This recipe requires day-ahead preparation. *

2 cups chopped pecans
bourbon, *or* rum
1 cup butter
2 pounds powdered sugar
2 cups chocolate chips
1 ounce paraffin wax

Cover pecans with bourbon, *or* rum, and soak overnight.
Combine butter and powdered sugar.
Drain the pecans. (You may drink the liquid if you wish.)
Add pecans to the butter-sugar mixture. Mix well.
* Refrigerate overnight.

Roll into 1-inch balls, placing a toothpick in each ball. Place balls on a cookie sheet. Refrigerate at least 4 hours.
Melt chocolate chips with the paraffin.
Dip chilled balls into chocolate and place on waxed paper.
Remove toothpicks.
Refrigerate until solid.

Kiferlings

1 pound butter, softened
½ cup sugar
1½ cups ground almonds
1 teaspoon vanilla extract
4 cups flour
powdered sugar

Cooking time: 12 to 15 minutes

Cream butter and sugar.
Mix in the ground almonds and vanilla extract.
Add the flour a little at a time for easier mixing.
Form into one-inch balls. Place on baking sheet.
Bake at 350° for 12 to 15 minutes.
While cookies are warm, roll them in powdered sugar.
When cooled, roll in powdered sugar again.

More Across Colorado

View of Park County's Alma.

ALMA

Alma was born with mineral fever and never fully recovered. The initial symptoms - swarms of prospectors, a manic construction boom, and two short-lived smelters (among the first in Colorado) - disappeared soon after the town's founding in 1873, but the bug that produced them stayed in Alma's blood. The fever surged again in the 1880s, when a system based on high-pressure water hoses revived several dormant mines, and again during the Great Depression, when unemployed workers came here to sift through long-idled claims. Mines still open and close in this region depending on fluctuating mineral prices (as recently as the 1980s, mining was the largest private employer in Park County), though by 2000 Alma's economy depended primarily on tourism. Yet, its mining heritage remains much in evidence. There's gold and silver around Alma yet - and thus always the chance for another outbreak of the town's peculiar fever.

More Across Colorado

Lemon Angel Dessert

This recipe may require day-ahead preparation.*

Crust:
3 egg whites
1 cup sugar
1 teaspoon vanilla
1 cup Club Cracker crumbs
1 cup finely chopped pecans

Filling:
4 egg yolks
½ cup sugar
½ cup lemon juice
2 cups whipping cream
½ cup powdered sugar
½ cup toasted coconut

Cooking time: 20 to 40 minutes
Serves: 8 to 10

Crust:
Beat the egg whites till soft peaks form.
Add sugar and vanilla, and beat to hard peaks.
Fold in the cracker crumbs and pecans.
Place in a deep-dish pie plate and bake at 350° for 20 to 40 minutes, or until light brown. Cool.

Filling:
Beat the egg yolks until pale yellow.
Add sugar and lemon juice, and cook until thick.
Cool.
Whip cream and powdered sugar until soft peaks form.
Spread half of this mixture on the chilled crust.
Top with the lemon mixture.
Place in the refrigerator to let the top thicken.
Top with remaining whipped cream.
Sprinkle with toasted coconut.
* Chill for at least 6 hours before serving.

Cut into wedges to serve.

More Across Colorado

Fairplay-area hydraulic mining operation, late 1870s. In 1875, a Park County placer owner contracted for Chinese workers, and soon this company employed 100 Chinese. By 1882, the Chinese leased and worked their own claims.

More Across Colorado

MINING TECHNIQUES

Though folklore celebrates the lonely gold-rusher, toiling for his fortune with only a pick and tin pan, advances in mining technology quickly left him behind. His primitive placer diggings, which relied on running water to separate nuggets and gold dust from the river rock, were easy and cheap to implement but rarely made millionaires. The real fortunes lay deep underground. Unlocking them, however, required powerful explosives, industrial machinery, stamp mills, and railroad transport, along with a method (smelting) that applied heat and chemicals to distill the complex ores into pure metals. Such operations required an enormous investment of capital and expertise, but they produced ore by the ton and sometimes yielded commensurate profits. By the mid-1870s, just a few years after Colorado's first mineral strikes, the pick-swinging prospector had all but disappeared; most had abandoned their dreams of quick riches and taken wage-earning jobs in corporate mines.

Mocha Chiffon Pie

10-inch baked pie shell, *or* 2 8-inch baked
     shells
1 tablespoon plain gelatin
¼ cup cold water
⅓ cup cocoa – *not instant cocoa mix*
½ cup sugar
½ teaspoon salt
4 egg yolks, beaten
1 cup strong brewed coffee, cooled
1 teaspoon vanilla
4 egg whites, stiffly beaten
½ cup sugar
whipped cream
chopped nut meats

Cooking time: 2 hours
Serves: 8 to 10

Soften gelatin in cold water.
In top of double boiler or heavy pan, combine cocoa, sugar, salt,
egg yolks and coffee.
Cook, stirring constantly, until thickened.
Stir in gelatin and vanilla.
Cool thoroughly in refrigerator until mixture begins to set.
Beat egg whites until frothy, then add sugar very slowly until stiff
meringue is formed.
Fold gently into thickened cocoa mixture.
Pour into baked pie shell(s) and chill thoroughly.
Top with whipped cream and nut meats.

Note: Separate eggs when cold and allow the yolks and whites to
reach room temperature before beating to get maximum volume.

More Across Colorado

CONTINENTAL DIVIDE MAIL DELIVERY

Unidentified mail carrier, 1860s.
Just like the legendary Father Dyer,
this mailman made his rounds on
what were then known as snowshoes.
These primitive boards were heavy
and unwieldy, measuring ten feet in
length and an inch in thickness. The
single pole was used for balance and
braking.

More Across Colorado

Mousse au Chocolat

*Day-ahead preparation is preferable. ***

6 6-ounce squares of semi-sweet chocolate
3 tablespoons water
3 egg yolks
1 tablespoon butter
1 teaspoon vanilla
3 egg whites
½ cup heavy cream, whipped and sweetened

Cooking time: 10 minutes
Serves: 4 to 6

Place chocolate and water in a heavy saucepan over low heat, stirring constantly until chocolate is melted.

Drop egg yolks into chocolate, one at a time, stirring after each addition. Remove from the heat, and stir in butter and vanilla.

Beat egg whites into soft peaks, and then fold into chocolate mixture.

Pour into ramekins for individual servings, or into a bowl if filling is to be used with meringues.

* *Refrigerate, preferably overnight.*

Serve with a dollop of whipped cream.

Note: This can be served as a stand-alone dessert, or used as an alternative or additional filling for small dessert meringues.
See **Coffee Mousse in Meringue Shells** for meringue recipe.

More Across Colorado

Nestled at the base of Republican Mountain at the rear of this 1880s' photo is the Lebanon Mine, now restored. Visitors can tour this mine complex complete with an equipment shed, manager's office, changing room, blacksmith shop, and mill.

PRESERVING THE PAST

The Colorado Central Railroad lost the race to get to Leadville and thus missed out on that city's lucrative silver-ore freight traffic. But the four-mile stretch of track between Georgetown and Silver Plume proved almost as valuable as a tourist attraction. The segment traversed a steep, narrow canyon that defied conventional routing, requiring a tangle of hairpin turns and crisscrossing tracks, crowned by a 95-foot-high trestle dubbed the Georgetown Loop. Seven years in the making, the steel curlicue opened on March 10, 1884, and its ingenious design and spectacular views made it one of the engineering wonders of the world. Visitors came from across the globe to ride its rails. Though the Loop was dismantled in 1939 because of flagging ridership, preservationists understood its importance and worked to rebuild it in the 1970s. With the completion of the bridge in 1984, the Loop attracted a whole new generation of tourists.

More Across Colorado

Oatmeal Crispies

This recipe requires day-ahead preparation. *

1 cup shortening
1 cup brown sugar, packed
1 cup sugar
1 teaspoon vanilla extract
2 eggs, beaten
1½ cups flour
1 teaspoon salt
1 teaspoon soda
3 cups quick-cooking oats
½ cup finely chopped walnuts

Cooking time: 10 minutes
Yield: 4 dozen

Cream together the shortening and sugars.
Add vanilla and eggs, and beat well.
In separate bowl, mix flour, salt and soda.
Add dry ingredients to creamed mixture, along with oats and nutmeats.
Mix well; dough will be stiff.
Divide dough in half and form each half in a roll.
Place on wax paper and wrap tightly.
* *Place in refrigerator overnight.*

When ready to serve, preheat oven to 350°.
Slice dough into ½-inch slices and place on greased cookie sheet.
Bake at 350° for 10 minutes or until lightly browned.

Story: When I was a little girl, these were my favorite cookies. Our house burned, and the beloved recipe was lost – or so we thought. Many years after I was grown, as a Christmas gift for me, my father shelled a coffee can full of walnuts and placed inside the recipe that Mom had found. I have never forgotten what a wonderful gift that was that year! It has become a favorite cookie to my family.
Joanne H. Johnson

More Across Colorado

SILVER PLUME

Silver Plume photographed from Sunrise Peak, c. 1890. The use of lumber for mines, buildings, and fuel left the area's hillsides barren and made the slopes prone to rock and snow slides.

With its smaller buildings and homes, Silver Plume (incorporated in 1880) had little of the elegance of neighboring Georgetown. What it did have was mines: More than forty of them, and several hundred claims, with strange names (including the Terrible and the 7:30) but terrific outputs. Many of the profits flowed two miles downhill to Georgetown, where a number of mine owners lived, but Silver Plume's 2,000 inhabitants, mostly rank-and-file mine workers (many of them recent European immigrants), had their own assets; these included a newspaper, a brewery, and the 7:30 mine's beloved cornet band. The town also featured marvelous engineering, with roads and mills built into the steepest cliffs imaginable. There was nothing fancy about the place, but Silver Plume embodied the essence of Colorado mining towns: Optimism and opportunity, with the promise of untold fortune.

More Across Colorado

Old-Fashioned Butter Cookies

3 cups flour
1 teaspoon baking powder
½ teaspoon salt
1 cup butter
¾ cup sugar
1 egg
2 tablespoons milk, *or* cream
1 teaspoon vanilla
optional decorations: cookie decors, sugar, *or*
      icing

Cooking time: 5 to 8 minutes
Yield: 3 dozen

Sift flour with baking powder and salt. Set aside.
Cream the butter.
Gradually add sugar, creaming well.
Add egg, milk *or* cream, and vanilla.
Add dry ingredients gradually; mix well.
Chill dough.
Roll out one-third of dough at a time on floured surface to quarter-inch thickness.
Cut into desired shapes.
Place on ungreased cookie sheets.
Bake at 400° for 5 to 8 minutes until delicately browned.
May decorate with cookie decors, sugar, *or* icing.

Story: I grew up in a German bakery in Baltimore, Maryland. It was located across the street from an old slave market, which is now a city market, Hollins Market. This is my father's sugar cookie recipe that he learned at baker's school in Germany. *Em Broughton*

More Across Colorado

GEORGETOWN

By the mid-1870s, nearly 5,000 people lived in Georgetown, making it the third-largest settlement in Colorado Territory.

The gold seekers who founded Georgetown in 1859 stayed only four years, extracting limited amounts of gold, never fully realizing that a silver bonanza lay under their feet. The white metal was this valley's treasure, streaking the mountains in such abundance that Georgetown soon became famous as the Silver Queen. It was royal indeed, with platted streets, elegant hotels, cultural societies, and tidy homes. But Georgetown suffered from the absence of rail service, which made shipping costly and time consuming. Ironically, when the Colorado Central Railroad finally did reach town in 1877, the city barely had time to enjoy it: Leadville's spectacular mineral strikes the following year made it Colorado's new silver champion. Trumped but not tarnished, Georgetown continued to produce steady yields through the Silver Panic of 1893, a remarkable twenty-nine-year run of prosperity.

More Across Colorado

Old-Fashioned Sugar Cream Pie

2 baked 9-inch pie shells, *or* 1 baked 10-inch
      deep-dish shell
3 cups half-and-half cream
¾ cup butter
1½ cups sugar
salt to taste
⅓ heaping cup cornstarch (or more)
½ cup milk
2 teaspoons vanilla extract
1 teaspoon nutmeg
additional nutmeg

Toppings, optional:
toasted coconut
toasted slivered almonds

Cooking time: 30 minutes
Serves: 12 (2 pies)

Melt the butter in the half-and-half.
Combine the sugar, salt, cornstarch and milk.
Add to the half-and-half mixture.
Cook and stir constantly until it thickens – about 25 minutes.
Add vanilla and nutmeg.
Pour into 2 baked pie shells, *or* 1 deep-dish shell.
Sprinkle with a little nutmeg and bake at 350° for 5 minutes.

More Across Colorado

More Across Colorado

MOUNTAIN ROAD BUILDING

Colorado's early mountain motorists rattled along at a few miles per hour, content merely to keep their wheels on the road. Those high-country routes generally followed old wagon trails and lacked drainage, grading, and paved surfaces. The 1910s brought scattered improvements, but modern roads remained scarce until the 1930s, when Charles Vail became state highway chief. During his tenure (1930 - 1945), Colorado's paved highway mileage increased from 500 to 5,000, shortening travel times from days to hours and unifying the state's economy. The interstate highways (begun in the 1950s) and Eisenhower Tunnel (opened in 1973) propelled Colorado's tourism and ski industries and revitalized stagnant local economies. Still, there never seemed to be enough roads. By the 1990s, traffic was a chronic concern, posing new challenges to the masters of mountain mobility.

By going beneath the Continental Divide, the Eisenhower Tunnel became Colorado's most reliable East-West mountain route. The westbound tunnel (shown under construction in 1970) was named for President Eisenhower. In 1979 an eastern bore was completed and named for Edwin Johnson, a former Colorado governor and U.S. senator.

Pumpkin Chocolate Chip Cake

4 eggs
2 cups sugar
3 cups flour (plus 2 tablespoons for high
      altitude)
½ teaspoon salt
⅔ cup oil
½ teaspoon cinnamon
1 cup chocolate chips
2 cups pumpkin (15-ounce to 16-ounce can)
2 teaspoons baking powder
2 teaspoons baking soda

Cooking time: about 55 minutes
Serves: 15

Preheat oven to 350°.
Grease Bundt pan.
Combine all ingredients, stirring until well blended.
Pour into prepared pan and bake for approximately 55 minutes.
Let cool for 20 minutes before removing from pan.

Note: Applesauce can be substituted for the oil for a low-fat version.

Story: I received this recipe from the Brickhouse Inn, a bed-and-breakfast I always stay at in Gettysburg, Pennsylvania. The inn owner was testing the recipe and gave me a piece to take out on my battlefield hike. It was wonderful! And when she put it out for the guests on my high marks, it was gobbled up by everyone. I had to have the recipe, and everyone I have given a piece to has enjoyed it as well. A great fall recipe! *Chris Geddes*

More Across Colorado

This is believed to be a view of Dillon's Main Street.

DILLON AND THE DAM

A tale of four towns underlies Dillon. Founded in 1873, the town moved in 1882 to greet the advancing Denver & Rio Grande tracks. A month later the Denver, South Park & Pacific arrived, and Dillon moved again, buildings and all - a move that allowed both railroads to pass through town. There it rested for the next seventy-nine years, a sleepy, picturesque hamlet of ranchers and merchants. In 1961 construction began on Dillon Dam, forcing yet another relocation. Several of the town's buildings were uprooted and relocated to higher ground at Breckenridge, Silverthorne, and Frisco. At least nine homes and several businesses were moved to the new Dillon townsite, where residents pieced their community back together for its fourth incarnation. The three former Dillon townsites now lie 250 feet beneath the surface of the reservoir.

 *More Across Colorado*

Raspberry Swirl

This recipe requires day-ahead preparation. *

Crust:
6 tablespoons. butter, melted
1½ cups graham cracker crumbs
4 tablespoons sugar

Filling:
6 egg yolks
2 8-ounce packages cream cheese, softened
2 cups sugar
6 egg whites
2 cups whipping cream, *or* 8 ounces frozen
      whipped topping, thawed
10-ounce box frozen raspberries, partially
      thawed

Serves: 12 to 15

Crust:
Combine melted butter, graham cracker crumbs and the sugar.
Reserve 1 tablespoon crumb mixture for the top.
Lightly press into a well-greased 9x13-inch pan.
Refrigerate for 15 minutes.

Filling:
Beat egg yolks until thickened.
Add cream cheese and sugar, beating until smooth and light.
Beat egg whites until stiff peaks form; set aside.
Whip the cream.
Fold egg whites and whipped cream, *or* whipped topping, into the cream cheese mixture.
Drain the raspberries and strain to remove seeds.
Crush the berries into a purée.
Gently swirl half of the purée into the cheese filling and spread over the graham cracker crust.
With a knife, gently swirl the remaining purée into the filling.
Freeze until solid – overnight.

Serve frozen, cut into squares.

More Across Colorado

Mount of the Holy Cross, William Henry Jackson, 1873.

MOUNT OF THE HOLY CROSS

"It is as if God has set His sign, His seal, His promise there - a beacon upon the very center and height of the Continent to all its people and all its generations . . . as if here was a great supply store and workshop of Creation, the fountain of Earth." Samuel Bowles, *The Switzerland of America* (1869).

A cross of snow, shining on a mountainside? Surely just a wilderness mirage. But this rumor (which began circulating in the 1860s) proved true. The 1,500-foot-tall marvel, mapped and photographed by Frederick Hayden's 1873 survey team, struck a chord deep in the nation's imagination. Poets and painters immortalized it, while hordes of pilgrims trekked westward to see for themselves what must be a divine portent. The difficulty of the journey only made it more meaningful; this was a trial of faith. Shrine Pass Road, dedicated in 1931, brought such a flood of believers that President Herbert Hoover was compelled to place the site under federal management. Years of weathering have blurred the image somewhat, but it remains a miraculous sight - a glimmer of redemption, lifting spirits skyward.

More Across Colorado

Sherry Cake

*This recipe gains in flavor if prepared 1 to 2 days ahead. ***

1 package yellow cake mix
1 package instant vanilla pudding (small box)
¾ cup golden cream sherry
¾ cup oil
4 eggs
1 teaspoon nutmeg
⅛ cup poppy seeds, optional
Cooking time: 45 to 50 minutes
Serves: 12

Preheat oven to 350°. In large mixing bowl, combine all ingredients. Mix on electric mixer's low speed until all ingredients are moistened. Beat on medium-high for 4 minutes. Grease and flour a Bundt pan of 10 to 12 cups. Pour batter into pan. Bake at 350° for 45 to 50 minutes, or until a toothpick comes out clean. Leave cake in pan for 20 minutes, then dust with powdered sugar while warm.

* This cake will increase in flavor if wrapped tightly and kept for a day or two before serving.

Sour Cream Cookies

2 cups sugar
½ cup *each* shortening and butter
3 eggs
1 cup sour cream
2 teaspoons vanilla extract
1½ teaspoons baking soda
½ teaspoon salt
4½ cups flour
sugar

Cooking time: 8 to 10 minutes
Yield: 4 dozen

Mix first 6 ingredients until creamy. Add remaining ingredients. Once dough is mixed, place bowl in refrigerator for about 1 hour. When dough is chilled, roll out to about quarter-inch thickness. Cut with favorite cookie cutter. Place on baking sheet, sprinkle lightly with sugar. Bake at 375° for 8 to 10 minutes, until lightly browned.

Story: This is my Grandma Hallene's favorite cookie recipe. She made these whenever we would visit the family's Peters 313 Ranch in northeastern Colorado. Now my mom makes them for her grandchildren. *Angela Caudill*

More Across Colorado

GRANITE

Granite was an early seat of Lake County, one of the two largest of Colorado Territory's seventeen original jurisdictions; it included all or part of fourteen present-day counties. As settlement expanded, the map splintered into increasingly smaller portions: the seventeen counties had become forty-six by 1889 and sixty-three by 1913. Mineral strikes, land cultivation, railroad development, and Indian treaties fueled this increase in boundary drawing, which was both a reflection of demographic trends and a means of distributing power and patronage. County seats rose and fell in sync with mining fortunes. Granite, for example, succeeded two busted neighbors (Oro City and Dayton) as the Lake County seat, but was later usurped by silver-rich Leadville. (Granite remained the county seat for newly created Chaffee County but only until 1880.) After 1913 the state's tally of counties held steady until 1998, when voters approved the creation of Broomfield County, Colorado's sixty-fourth.

When this 1883 photo was taken, Granite was part of Chaffee County. The former Lake County Courthouse where Justice Dyer met his fateful end is the fifth building from the lower left.

More Across Colorado

Stove-Top Custard

3 egg yolks
¼ cup sugar
⅛ teaspoon salt
2 cups scalded milk
½ teaspoon vanilla extract
whipped cream

Cooking time: 20 to 30 minutes
Yield: 4 one-half-cup servings

In double-boiler over simmering water, beat egg yolks with fork.
Add the sugar and salt.
Gradually whisk in the warm scalded milk.
Cook and stir until the mixture coats a spoon, for 20 to 30 minutes.
Strain into a refrigerator dish. Press plastic wrap on top of custard to prevent skin forming. Chill.
Stir in the vanilla.
Serve with whipped cream.

Story: This comes from the Norwegian side of the family. I loved it when I was sick. *Susan Johnson*

Sugary Spicy Pecans

1 egg white
1 tablespoon water
2 cups large pecan halves
1 cup sugar
dash of salt
1 teaspoon cinnamon
¼ teaspoon **each** ground ginger and nutmeg
dash of ground cloves

Cooking time: 45 minutes
Yield: 2 cups

Beat egg white and water until frothy, mix well with pecans.
Combine sugar, salt and spices.
Mix well with pecan mixture.
Spread on cookie sheet.
Bake at 225° for 45 minutes.
Stir occasionally.
Cool and store in sealed container.

More Across Colorado

Pack train, Hagerman Pass, 1870s.

MOUNTAIN TRANSPORTATION

Leadville-bound miners of the mid-1800s had their choice of roads through the formidable Mosquito Range, but all of them long, difficult, and hazardous. Mosquito Pass offered the most direct route from Denver, but at 13,188 feet it was steep and often buried in snow. Trout Creek Pass, though lower and easier, required a sixty-five-mile detour. Most travelers opted for the Tarryall and Arkansas Wagon Road, which crossed 11,900-foot Weston Pass and emerged at the mouth of Union Creek. Leadville's silver-mining boom brought an unbroken stream of wagons, pack trains, and stagecoaches. Though the wagon ruts are no longer visible, the old roadbed is quite evident across the Arkansas River as one drives along US 24.

More Across Colorado

Sweet Peanut Treat

2 cups (12 ounces) semi-sweet chocolate chips
10-ounce package butterscotch-flavored chips
18-ounce jar creamy peanut butter
16-ounce can cocktail peanuts
5-ounce can evaporated milk
1 cup sweet, unsalted butter
¼ cup vanilla pudding mix (half of 3-ounce
        package)
2 16-ounce packages powdered sugar, sifted

Cooking time: 30 minutes
Yield: 120 pieces

Butter a 15x10x1-inch pan.
Combine first 3 ingredients in a heavy pan.
Cook over low heat, stirring constantly, until smooth.
Pour half of chocolate mixture into prepared pan.
Refrigerate 20 minutes.
Combine the remaining chocolate mixture and peanuts, stirring well.
Set aside.
Combine the canned milk, butter and pudding mix in a saucepan.
Bring to a boil over medium heat; stir occasionally.
Reduce heat and simmer 2 minutes.
Mixture may look curdled, but that's okay.
Remove from heat.
Add sifted powdered sugar, and stir until smooth.
Spread over chilled chocolate mixture.
Then carefully spread the chocolate-peanut mixture on top.
Cover and refrigerate at least 1 hour, until firm.
Cut into small squares.
Store in refrigerator.

More Across Colorado

THE COAL MINERS

Crested Butte's early miners were mostly Anglo-Saxons from Cornwall, Wales, Scotland, and Ireland. This changed in the 1890s when the mines were worked by cheap labor drawn from southern Europe: Slavs, Greeks, and Italians. Unable to speak English, penniless, and new to coal mining, these immigrants were viewed by their Anglo-Saxon counterparts as rivals in a limited job market. They also faced exploitation in the mines, where safety precautions were more a distant hope than a reality. Still, they stayed on, giving Crested Butte an ethnic diversity unknown in many mining camps. They may have come poor, but as one immigrant proclaimed: "We came not empty-handed but brought a rich inheritance."

Joe Slota, second-generation Slovak.

More Across Colorado

Tipsy Chocolate Chip Cookies

1 cup sweet unsalted butter, room temperature
¾ cup white sugar
¾ cup brown sugar, firmly packed
1 tablespoon vanilla extract
1 tablespoon hazelnut liqueur (Frangelico)
1 tablespoon coffee liqueur (Kahlua)
2 large eggs
2¾ cups flour
1 teaspoon baking soda
½ teaspoon salt
2 11½-ounce packages milk chocolate chips
1 cup chopped walnuts
½ cup chopped pecans
½ cup chopped macadamia nuts

Cooking time: 12 to 14 minutes
Yield: 54 cookies

Preheat oven to 350°.
Using electric mixer, beat butter, sugars, vanilla and liqueurs until mixture is light and fluffy.
Add eggs and beat well.
Mix flour, baking soda and salt in a small bowl with a wire whisk.
Stir into butter mixture.
Mix in the chocolate chips and all nuts.
Drop batter, one-eighth of a cupful per cookie, onto ungreased cookie sheets, well spaced.
Bake until cookies are golden brown, 12 to 14 minutes.
Transfer to a wire rack and cool

More Across Colorado

CROSSROADS OF THE ROCKIES

Salida, 1880s.

In 1880, the stagecoach trip from Canon City to Leadville took twenty-six hours. That was something of a speed record for the Arkansas River road, once a trail, which by then was centuries old. The Utes had traveled it seasonally, pursuing the buffalo between South Park and the San Luis Valley, and Juan Bautista de Anza followed it in 1779, making the first recorded crossing of Poncha Pass in the process. With the mineral strikes of the 1870s, the bend of the Arkansas at Salida came to resemble Grand Central Station, funneling traffic north to Aspen and Leadville, west toward Telluride and Silverton, and south to the San Luis Valley and into New Mexico. Today it takes only a few hours to drive from Canon City to Leadville, but the route was generations in the making.

More Across Colorado

Tozzetti

½ cup chopped dried apricots, optional
¼ cup brandy, optional
4 eggs
2½ cups sugar
1 teaspoon vanilla, *or* almond extract
2 teaspoons baking powder
4 cups (at the most) flour
1½ cups whole almonds
1 egg, whipped

Cooking time: 30 to 40 minutes
Serves: 20

If adding the apricots, soak them in the brandy for half an hour ahead.

Combine eggs, sugar and vanilla. In a sifter, add baking powder to 1 cup of the flour. Add to egg mixture. Using a mixer, add enough flour to form a stiff dough. Add nuts and the apricots, if using.

Then flour a board and knead as you add more flour. Add flour *very slowly*, up to a total of 4 cups.

When dough is well-mixed – till it feels a little sticky, but not to the point it sticks to your palms – mold into 3 long, thin, high loaves on a well-buttered cookie sheet. Brush well with a whipped egg.

Bake at 375° for 30 to 40 minutes, until the loaves are brown. Remove from cookie sheet, cut immediately on an angle, separate and let cool. They keep very well in the freezer.

Story: This recipe is similar to the one I learned in Tuscany, but I have adjusted it to my own baking methods; the brandied apricots are definitely my own idea. As a birthday present six years ago, my husband gave me a trip to Chef Mariella Pellegrini's cooking class at the Antico Casale inn in Scanzano. I went with our daughter Peggy Smith, who lives in Fort Collins. We cooked in the mornings, with 6 to 8 other students at any one time – and toured Tuscany in the afternoons. *Annette Fricke*

More Across Colorado

The Denver, Leadville & Gunnison Railroad (formerly the Denver, South Park & Pacific) at the Palisade, on the west side of the Alpine Tunnel, 1890s.

THE ALPINE TUNNEL

It would be one of the world's toughest one-third mile of railroad track. In the race against the Denver & Rio Grande Railway to reach Gunnison, the Denver, South Park & Pacific Railroad gambled that a tunnel through the Continental Divide and Altman Pass (present-day Alpine Pass) would give the edge for victory. Work began in January 1880, but the 11,500-foot elevation, subzero temperatures, and crumbling rock slowed construction. Not until September 1882 did Denver, South Park & Pacific trains roll through the 1,772-foot tunnel and into Gunnison - a year later than its rival. Still, it is remarkable that the tunnel was completed at all, and that it was completed with an engineering error of less than one foot is astounding.

More Across Colorado

Unique Fresh Peach Pie

3 egg whites (at room temperature)
1 cup sugar
14 soda crackers
¼ teaspoon baking powder
⅓ cup finely chopped pecans, optional
1 tablespoon vanilla extract
12-ounce container Cool Whip
5 to 6 ripe peaches

Cooking time: 30 minutes
Serves: 6 to 8

Use a well-buttered 9-inch, *or* 10-inch, pie pan.
Beat egg whites until stiff, gradually beating in sugar until soft peaks form.
Roll crackers into fine crumbs.
Fold gently into egg whites, along with baking powder.
Fold in pecans, if using, and vanilla.
Spoon into pie pan.
Bake at 325° for 30 minutes.
Cool.
The crust will rise and then drop.
Dip peaches in boiling water for 2 to 2½ minutes.
Peel and slice the peaches directly into the crust.
Top with Cool Whip.
Chill in refrigerator several hours before serving.

More Across Colorado

Captain John W. Gunnison

GUNNISON EXPEDITION

In 1853 Capt. John W. Gunnison (1812-1853) led a survey party through the Central Rockies to find a possible route for the proposed transcontinental railroad. After he easily crossed Cochetopa Pass, Gunnison in September encountered the 2,500-foot gorge of the Black Canyon. Despite the breathtakingly sheer walls, the roar of the water, and the canyon's prevailing darkness, the survey party attempted to cross the abyss. But as the wagons were lowered by rope, two of them somersaulted and became, according to an observer, "true invalids." All this convinced Gunnison that building a railroad through these canyons was impossible.

More Across Colorado

Zucchini Dessert Squares

Crust:
2 cups flour
2 cups quick-cooking oatmeal
1½ cups sugar
½ teaspoon cinnamon
½ teaspoon salt
1 cup cold butter

Filling:
8 to 10 cups (4 to 5 pounds) peeled, seeded and
     sliced zucchini
⅔ cup lemon juice
1 cup sugar
1 teaspoon cinnamon
1 teaspoon nutmeg

Cooking time: 52 to 57 minutes
Serves: 16 to 20

Grease a 13x9x2-inch baking pan.
Measure dry ingredients into mixing bowl.
Cut in the butter until mixture is crumbly.
Reserve 3 cups.
Pat remaining crumb mixture into bottom of prepared pan.
Bake at 375° for 12 minutes.

Filling:
Prepare filling while crust is baking.
Place prepared zucchini and lemon juice in a saucepan; bring to boil, reduce heat, cover and cook for 6 to 8 minutes, till crisp-tender. Stir in the sugar, cinnamon and nutmeg.
Cover and simmer for 5 minutes; mixture will be thin.
Spoon filling over baked crust. Sprinkle reserved crumb mixture over the top.
Bake at 375° for 40 to 45 minutes, or until golden.

Story: Every summer we harvest many zucchini, and though I use them in almost everything I cook, when I came across this recipe, I had to try it. I've adjusted it somewhat to my own preference and method of preparing it. Whenever I take it to a potluck, I'm always asked for the recipe. In 2003, at the Arvada Harvest Festival, the recipe won first place in the Pie Category. *Lucille Lotito Pesce*

More Across Colorado

Teriyaki Quail, The Fort Restaurant, Morrison, Colorado

The West was built in good part by Chinese and Japanese immigrants who supplied both hands and brains to build railroads and cities, ranches and farms. Also, some of the first trappers who had been brought to our Northwest Coast by John Jacob Astor were Hawaiians. It is not surprising, therefore, that teriyaki came to the West early on.

Teriyaki Quail is accompanied by a grilled buffalo filet and elk medallion in The Fort's most popular entrée, The Game Plate. Lightly season the filet and medallion with salt and pepper, then grill over an open flame to rare or medium rare. And here's the recipe for the quail. It serves 10.

Dr. Sam'l P. Arnold, founder of The Fort Restaurant in Morrison, strumming his mandolin.
Photo by Tom Noel.

Marinade:

1 cup soy sauce
½ cup rice wine or dry sherry
¼ cup sugar
2 tablespoons minced fresh ginger
3 cloves garlic, minced
2 whole star anise
¼ cup finely chopped orange peel
1 cup orange juice
1 cup water
8 2½ to 3½-ounce partially deboned quail
4 orange slices for garnish

Combine all marinade ingredients in a saucepan and bring to a boil over high heat. Lower the heat and simmer for 5 minutes. Let cool.

Place the quail in a single layer in a pan, pour the marinade over it, and let the quail marinate for 2 to 4 hours. Beware of leaving the birds in for more that 8 hours, because they will become unpalatably salty.

When ready to cook, heat the grill to medium or pre-heat the broiler. Cook the quail for 3 to 4 minutes on each side. Garnish with a twisted orange slice.

Yours for shinin' times in Colorado kitchens!

More Across Colorado

Ann Landers Meat Loaf

2 pounds extra-lean ground beef
1½ cups fine bread crumbs
2 eggs
¾ cup ketchup
½ cup warm water
1 envelope onion soup mix
8-ounce can tomato sauce

Cooking time: 1 hour to 1¼ hours
Serves: 8

Combine all ingredients except tomato sauce.
Place mixture in large (8½x4½x2½-inch) greased loaf pan.
Pour the tomato sauce over the loaf.
Bake at 350° for 1 hour to 1¼ hours.

Note: This freezes well.

Story: This recipe was an Ann Landers favorite, which she shared in her column about 20 years ago.

More Across Colorado

Until railroads superseded wagon travel in the late 1870s, over 150 wagons and coaches crossed daily over Mosquito Pass into and out of Leadville.

UTE HUNTING TRAILS

Many of the roads through the Rockies began as Ute hunting trails and were widened for freight traffic during the mineral booms of the 1860s. These rubble-strewn routes made for tedious going; one early traveler complained that after a full day's travel she could still see the embers from the previous night's campfire. That changed in 1880, when the first Denver & Rio Grande train steamed into Leadville, condensing a days-long ordeal into an hours-long excursion. Two other railroads soon pushed into the Upper Arkansas Valley, and by the 1920s motorists were driving along 40 South (precursor to US 24), one of the first paved highways across the mountains. But for all the advances in travel technology, the original routes have scarcely been improved upon; somewhere deep beneath the asphalt, the Utes' footprints still linger.

More Across Colorado

Beef Stroganoff

1½ pounds beef sirloin
½ to ¾ cup flour
salt, to taste
pepper, to taste
1 tablespoon butter
1 tablespoon olive oil (enough to cover bottom
     of pan)
1½ cups finely chopped onions
1 cup sliced fresh mushrooms
1 clove minced garlic
⅛ teaspoon nutmeg
1 can beef broth
1 bay leaf
1 cup red *or* white wine, *or* more, if desired
1 cup sour cream
white and wild rices, *or* noodles

Cooking time: 2 hours
Serves: 6

Trim fat from meat and cut into quarter-inch strips. Dredge meat in flour, salt and pepper. Set aside.

Melt butter in a hot skillet; add olive oil to barely cover pan bottom. Sauté onions, then add mushrooms, garlic and nutmeg.

Remove from pan to a bowl and set aside.

Using same pan, add the prepared meat, quickly browning on all sides.

Add the beef broth and the sautéed vegetables.

Add bay leaf – remember to remove before serving – and wine. Slowly cook, uncovered, until liquid is reduced and has started to thicken.

Cover and cook on low, just barely simmering, until meat is tender – 30 to 45 minutes.

Stir occasionally, scraping the bottom of the pan to loosen bits of meat that may have become stuck.

Remove sour cream from the refrigerator so it will not be too cold when added to the meat mixture.

When meat is tender, remove from heat and add sour cream, stirring constantly. ***Do not boil as cream will curdle***.

Heat for about 3 minutes.

Serve over a blend of white and wild rice, *or* noodles.

More Across Colorado

CONTINENTAL DIVIDE NATIONAL SCENIC TRAIL

Though today this highway is known as US 24, it started off as part of the transcontinental Pikes Peak Ocean to Ocean highway. Through Granite, the road follows the old Colorado Midland Railroad grade.

More Across Colorado

Early travelers dreaded the forbidding Continental Divide (the high mountains separating the Atlantic and Pacific watersheds). Later settlers viewed it as a challenge to be conquered: Road builders surmounted it, railroaders tunneled through it, and engineers diverted Western Slope water underneath it to irrigate farms and sustain cities in eastern Colorado. But the Continental Divide Trail, which Congress designated a National Scenic Trail in 1978, simply takes the landmark on its own terms. When finished, the trail will travel 3,100 miles along the nation's crest across five states, winding through 800 miles of Colorado wilderness. The route often diverges from the Divide proper as some portions are simply too rugged for travel. And therein lies the Divide's mystique: Though mapped and breached, it remains somehow impenetrable, one of the nation's last unspoiled places.

Cheese-Topped Pork Chops

1 tablespoon oil
6 pork chops, ½-inch thick
2 tablespoons butter
⅓ cup flour
⅔ cup milk
1 beaten egg
2 tablespoons finely chopped onions
½ cup grated Parmesan cheese
⅛ teaspoon pepper
3 tablespoons dried parsley flakes

Cooking time: 40 to 45 minutes
Serves: 6

Preheat oven to 350°.
Heat the oil in a large skillet over medium heat.
Brown pork chops.
Arrange the pork chops in an ungreased 9x13-inch baking dish. Set aside.
Melt the butter in a small saucepan over low heat.
Stir in the flour.
Gradually add the milk.
Cook until mixture thickens, stirring constantly. Mixture will thicken quickly.
Remove from heat, and stir in the beaten egg.
Add remaining ingredients, blending well.
Spoon the cheese mixture over the chops and tightly cover the baking dish with aluminum foil.
Bake at 350° for 30 minutes.
Uncover baking dish and bake for 10 to 15 minutes more, or until chops are tender.

More Across Colorado

Mount Princeton c. 1915.

More Across Colorado

THE ROOF OF THE ROCKIES

"The Colorado Rockies were once a great barrier to Western travel; then they became a great goal of Western travel." William M. Bueler, *Roof of the Rockies*.

Of the 68 Fourteeners - 14,000-foot-high mountains - in the continental United States, 54 are in Colorado, and 15 stand in the Sawatch Range. Miners swarmed over this line of Olympian alps from 1860 on; oblivious to the altitude, they went where the paydirt took them. With the rise of recreational mountaineering, the Fourteeners themselves became the prize, and the Sawatch Range (which includes the three highest peaks in the Rockies) represented the ultimate hiking and climbing experience. Over time, however, the steadily increasing backpacking and hiking traffic began to cause erosion, soil compaction, and vegetation damage, and land managers began warning of environmental degradation. With several hundred thousand hikers a year, the Fourteeners are in danger of being loved to death.

Chicken and Chipped Beef

8 chicken breast halves, boneless, skinless
8 slices bacon
1 package chipped beef
1 cup sour cream
1 can cream of mushroom soup

Cooking time: 3 hours
Serves: 8

Grease a 9x13-inch baking dish.
Wrap chicken breasts in bacon.
Shred the chipped beef into bottom of the prepared dish.
Place chicken breasts on top of chipped beef.
Combine sour cream and soup, and spread over the top.
Bake at 275° for 3 hours.

Chicken Breast Supreme

6 to 8 boneless, skinless chicken breast halves,
        flattened to uniform thickness
1 envelope dry Italian salad dressing mix
1 can cream of golden mushroom soup
1 can cream of mushroom soup with roasted
        garlic
8-ounce package cream cheese, softened
8-ounce carton sour cream with chives

Cooking time: 1 hour
Serves: 6 to 8

Place chicken in a 9x13-inch greased baking dish.
Sprinkle Italian dressing over the chicken.
Mix soups, sour cream and cream cheese until smooth.
Spread over the chicken.
Bake at 350° for 1 hour.
Serve with rice.

More Across Colorado

St. Elmo

More Across Colorado

CITIES IN THE WILDERNESS

Rome wasn't built in a day, but Chaffee City ... well, maybe. From 1879 to 1890, hardly a week passed without the rise of another town in the surrounding hills. All it took was a decent mineral strike or a promising railroad survey, and banks, saloons, and hardware stores would sprout like weeds in a storm-washed meadow. The more ambitious communities added cosmopolitan flourishes such as newspapers and brass bands. These "instant cities" embodied the ingenuity of a pioneering nation, its sheer creative energy. That most of them collapsed within a few years is beside the point. The town builders believed they could build great cities in the wilderness - powerful testimony to the force of the American Dream.

Alpine *was* a gust of wind, arriving with great force, then vanishing with hardly a trace. Founded in 1879, the town gained 2,000 citizens in a matter of weeks; when the railroad tracks reached neighboring St. Elmo a few years later, all but two left. The same thing happened over and over in Colorado. Along the Upper Arkansas, Arbourville, Calumet, Harvard City, Romley, Silverdale, Winfield, Turrett, and dozens of other towns sprang into being, only to be crushed by the Silver Panic of 1893, or a fire, or competition from a rival settlement. St. Elmo, the town that killed Alpine, hung on until the 1950s, and its skeleton remains quite intact; other lost cities are marked only by a cemetery, a town dump, maybe just a ghostly breeze.

Chicken Cacciatore

4 cloves garlic
2 teaspoons fresh rosemary
½ teaspoon kosher salt
3 tablespoons olive oil (more, as needed)
6 chicken skin-on drumsticks
6 chicken skin-on thighs
4 chicken skin-on breast halves
1 medium onion, chopped
¾ cup chopped carrot
2 celery stalks, chopped
2 cloves garlic, minced
8 ounces fresh button mushrooms, sliced
28-ounce can crushed plum tomatoes, packed in
     purée
2 teaspoons chopped fresh oregano
1 cup dry red wine
16 Kalamata olives, pitted and chopped
salt and/or pepper, to taste

Cooking time: 1 hour and 15 minutes
Serves: 8

Combine the garlic, rosemary and salt in a food processor until a paste is formed.
Spread a bit of the paste on the skin side of each chicken piece.
Let the pieces marinate for about 1 hour.
Pour oil into a Dutch oven, heat and brown both sides of the chicken pieces – about 6 minutes on each side.
Remove chicken pieces to a platter.
Add onion, carrot, celery and garlic to Dutch oven – with additional olive oil, if necessary – and cook until soft.
Add mushrooms and cook until soft.
Add tomatoes, chopped oregano and red wine, stirring to mix well.
Cook on medium-high heat for about 10 minutes, to reduce liquid.
Place the chicken pieces back in the pot, partially covering the pot.
Add olives.
Reduce heat to low simmer and cook for an additional 45 minutes until the chicken is thoroughly cooked, and the flavors are blended.
Add salt and/or pepper, as needed.

More Across Colorado

148

Crested Butte

CRESTED BUTTE

In the early 1860s, prospectors crowded the Elk Mountains, searching for precious metals. But neither gold nor silver made Crested Butte famous. Instead, coal became king. Incorporated in 1880, Crested Butte grew quickly, especially after the Denver & Rio Grande trains rumbled into camp in 1881. By the summer of 1882, the town boasted a population of 1,000, three fine hotels, a bank, over a dozen saloons, five sawmills, and a unique plaza that would soon hold three artificial lakes. Crested Butte remained a coal town until the last mine shut down in 1952.

More Across Colorado

Chicken Maryland

4 chicken breasts, boneless and skinless
3 tablespoons butter
2 tablespoons flour
1 cup light cream
2 cups sliced fresh mushrooms
2 tablespoons butter
½ teaspoon salt
⅛ teaspoon pepper
2 tablespoons cooking sherry

Cooking time: 20 minutes
Serves: 4

Place each chicken breast between sheets of plastic wrap and flatten to a quarter inch.
Sauté chicken breasts using 3 tablespoons of butter until brown and tender. Remove to a hot platter.
Using same skillet, stir in flour, add cream, and stir until thickened.
In another skillet, sauté mushrooms in 2 tablespoons butter.
Season with salt and pepper. Stir in sherry.
Add white sauce to mushroom mixture.
Serve sauce over chicken.

Chicken Sandwiches

2 3-ounce packages cream cheese
½ teaspoon salt
¼ teaspoon pepper
7-ounce can mushrooms, drained
2 cups cubed, cooked chicken
4 teaspoons chopped onion
2 8-ounce cans crescent rolls
4 tablespoons melted butter – more if needed
¾ cup crushed croutons

Combine first six ingredients. Separate rolls, press into 8 rectangles. Spoon about one-third cup of mixture onto center of each rectangle. Pull corners up and twist, completely enclosing the filling. Roll in the butter and dip into the crushed croutons.
Place on a cookie sheet. Bake at 350° for 25 to 30 minutes.

Yield: 8 sandwiches

More Across Colorado

FORT GARLAND

To protect the valley's Hispano settlers against Indian attacks, the U.S. Army established Fort Massachusetts in 1852 near Blanca Peak. But the fort was too remote to be effective, so in 1858 the Army put up a new post, Fort Garland. Built largely of adobe, the new fort stood guard over the San Luis Valley and its people until abandoned in 1883. The Colorado Historical Society invites you to visit Fort Garland, which has been preserved as a museum.

Soldiers lounging at Fort Garland.

More Across Colorado

Chicken Enchilada Casserole

1 can cream of mushroom soup
1 can cream of chicken soup
15-ounce can evaporated milk
½ cup finely chopped onion
4-ounce can diced green chiles
6-inch corn tortillas
2½ cups cooked diced chicken, *or* more to suit
   taste
12 ounces sharp cheddar, grated
salsa

Cooking time: 40 minutes
Serves: 6

Preheat oven to 350°.
Place soups, milk, onion and green chiles in blender and blend briefly but well.
Grease a 9x13-inch baking dish.
Cut each tortilla into 4 pieces.
Arrange 1 layer of tortillas on the bottom of the dish.
Spread half of the chicken over the tortillas.
Carefully spoon half of the soup mixture over the chicken layer.
Sprinkle with half of grated cheese.
Repeat layers, ending with cheese as top layer.
Bake at 350° for 40 minutes or until bubbly.
Remove from oven and let it set in warm place for 10 minutes before serving.
To serve, cut in squares.
Serve with salsa on the side.

More Across Colorado

Officers of the First Regiment, Colorado Volunteer Calvalry. Captain Charles Kerber, seated far right, settled the area around Villa Grove after his discharge from Fort Garland in 1865.

VILLA GROVE

First settled in 1865 by Colorado Civil War veterans, Villa Grove came down with a serious case of mining fever in 1880. Prospectors flooded the mountains to the west for a crack at the Bonanza Lode; no less a personage than Ulysses S. Grant came to inspect the diggings. Alas, the Bonanza proved anything but: Its low-grade silver ore made no millionaires, and by 1900 most miners had moved on. Better fortunes were found just east of town, where the Orient iron mine coughed up forty years' worth of paydirt. Though the mines have long since closed, Villa Grove (platted in 1882) still thrives as a picturesque village, serving ranchers, farmers, small businesses, and tourists.

More Across Colorado

Chinese Pepper Steak

1 tablespoon soy sauce
2 cloves garlic, minced
¼ cup vegetable oil
1 pound round steak, cut into 1-inch strips
1 large green pepper, cut into 1-inch strips
1 large sweet onion, sliced in ½-inch strips
½ cup angle-sliced celery
1 teaspoon cornstarch
¼ cup cold water

Cooking time: 15 to 18 minutes
Serves: 4

Combine soy sauce, garlic and oil, and pour over steak strips.
Marinate steak for 1 to 2 hours.
Heat wok, *or* frying pan, and brown meat, stirring occasionally.
Add pepper, onion and celery.
Cover and cook about 8 minutes over low heat.
Dissolve cornstarch in cold water and stir into the meat mixture until it thickens.
Simmer for another 5 to 10 minutes until meat is tender.
Serve over rice.

More Across Colorado

"I believe I can say with safety that no other locality with equal advantages can be found between the Gulf of Mexico and the British possessions."
Alexander Hunt, construction chief for the Denver & Rio Grande, 1877.

ALAMOSA

The first U.S. citizen known to have seen the site of present-day Alamosa, Lt. Zebulon M. Pike, was arrested nearby in 1807 for trespassing on Spanish soil. But the Spanish were trespassers themselves: the Utes occupied the land. The conflicting territorial claims were resolved after the Mexican War, when the United States acquired this region and before long forced the Utes westward. Founded by the Denver & Rio Grande Railway in 1878, Alamosa (Spanish for place of the cottonwood grove) soon emerged as a commercial center, providing essential services to the San Luis Valley's farmers and ranchers, and to miners in the San Juans. Today, Alamosa remains the dominant town for the entire region, continuing to serve farmers and ranchers, as well as college students, tourists, and outdoor recreationists.

More Across Colorado

Genuine Green Chile

4 pounds boneless pork loin, with fat and gristle
    removed, cut into 1-inch cubes
¾ tablespoon salt
4 tablespoons vegetable oil
2 tablespoons water
1 to 2 tablespoons vegetable shortening
1 bunch cilantro, chopped fine, no end stems
2 tablespoons vegetable oil
4 tablespoons flour
3 large garlic cloves, sliced thin and lengthwise
2 cups (18 to 22) Hatch's roasted chiles, peeled
    and chopped
2 28-ounce cans diced, peeled tomatoes
2 cups water
¾ tablespoon salt, *or* to taste
5 cups cooked, unseasoned white rice
stovetop-grilled flour, *or* wheat, tortillas

Cooking time: 4½ hours
Serves: 10

Combine first 4 ingredients in a 5-quart pan generously greased with vegetable shortening. Sauté, covered, until meat is no longer pink. Add cilantro. With a flat-tipped wooden spoon, stir and sauté until cilantro is limp but still green. Remove from heat, and cool, uncovered, for 15 minutes. Then add the 2 tablespoons of vegetable oil and mix well. Add flour and garlic, and mix well. Brown over medium heat, stirring occasionally so nothing sticks to pan bottom. When mixture shows good color, add chiles, blending gently. Add diced tomatoes and water, mixing thoroughly. Salt to taste. Bring to boil uncovered. Then cover, move to a back burner, and cook over low heat a couple of hours, stirring occasionally. Eventually it will get hot and bubbly, no matter how low the heat. **At this point, remove from heat and remove lid.** Once it has cooled thoroughly, stir, cover and cook for a couple of hours or until it's so thick the spoon stands up in it. Serve with unseasoned rice and/or tortillas.

Note: Lay in a store of Hatch's roasted chiles when the sellers are in town late summer through fall. Keep chiles in the thick bags the sellers put them in until totally chilled (24 hours or so), then divide contents into freezer bags and freeze. After defrosting the amount needed, run each chile under lukewarm water – the blackened skin will wash right off. Slit lengthwise and remove all seeds. Place on a cutting board to drain, then chop in ½-inch pieces.

More Across Colorado

Saguache, c. 1920. While the Ute word Saguache is popularly translated as "water by the blue earth place," the Ute language is a living entity and to-day's Southern Ute Tribe states its literal meaning as "water that comes from underground."

More Across Colorado

SAGUACHE

The land around Saguache (pronounced sah-WATCH) has been inhabited for thousands of years, first by unnamed nomads, later by the Utes (who camped here seasonally), and later still by Mexican traders bound for California on the Old Spanish Trail. Hispano farmers first settled the area in the early 1860s, followed by Anglos after the Civil War. By 1874, the year of its formal incorporation, Saguache anchored one of Colorado's most important agricultural regions, supplying the mining camps of the Arkansas Valley and the San Juan Mountains. Despite its prosperity and county-seat status, however, the town never obtained the railroad access that would have enabled it to grow. It nonetheless evolved into a leading cattle center and remains the county seat. Saguache today is one of Colorado's deepest-rooted towns, with ranches worked continuously since the late 1800s.

Grilled Flank Steak

This recipe requires all-day or overnight marinating. *

¾ cup vegetable oil
2 tablespoons vinegar
¼ cup soy sauce
2 tablespoons chopped green onion
1½ teaspoons ginger
¼ cup honey
1 chopped garlic clove, *or* 1 tablespoon garlic
    chips
1 flank steak, flattened

Cooking time: 14 to 16 minutes
Serves: 2 people per pound of meat

Mix all ingredients in a large Zip-Lock Bag.
Drop in the flattened flank steak and seal.
* *Marinate all day, **or** overnight, in the refrigerator, turning frequently.*

Grill for 7 to 8 minutes per side, depending on steak size and personal preference.
Slice across the grain diagonally, preferably with an electric knife.
A very low-calorie and low-fat entrée.

More Across Colorado

Hispano family in the San Luis Valley.

SAN LUIS VALLEY

In the 1840s, Hispanos from New Mexico began moving north to farm on Mexican land grants in the San Luis Valley. The communities they founded, beginning with San Luis in 1851, are today the oldest continuously inhabited towns in Colorado. Life in these settlements formed around *placitas:* A series of connected L-shaped, flat-roofed homes made of adobe, or logs covered with adobe. This was a reflection of the Southwest's architectural tradition. To support their crops and livestock, the settlers acquired Colorado's first known water rights, which date to 1852, and built the San Luis People's Ditch, the state's oldest operating irrigation system.

More Across Colorado

Ham and Noodle Casserole

12 ounces noodles, cooked and drained
1 medium onion, chopped
1 medium bell pepper, chopped
½ pound mushrooms, sliced, optional
4 tablespoons butter
1½ pounds cubed ham
5 to 8 ounces grated cheddar cheese
14.5-ounce can tomatoes, drained, broken up
2 cups sour cream
1 small can chopped black olives
salt to taste
pepper to taste
bread crumbs

Cooking time: 45 minutes
Serves: 12

Sauté the onion, bell pepper, and mushrooms if using, in the butter for 5 minutes.
Combine all ingredients except bread crumbs.
Place in a large greased baking dish.
Sprinkle top with bread crumbs.
Bake at 325° for 30 to 40 minutes – longer if prepared ahead and refrigerated.

More Across Colorado

Lake City, 1881.

METROPOLIS OF THE SAN JUANS

Gold strike in the San Juans! Word spread like wildfire that summer of 1874, and the following spring prospectors crowded into this high mountain valley. They pitched tents and erected log cabins with dirt floors and sod roofs. In August 1875, the town of Lake City, named for nearby Lake San Cristobal, was formed. As more and more families arrived, log cabins gave way to sturdy frame and brick homes. Soon general stores, hardware stores, barbershops, saloons, and hotels lined Silver Street. A school, library, opera house, and six churches sprang up. Within three years, boosters claimed the town had grown to 2,000 residents. The rough mining camp had become a full-fledged town - a gateway to the San Juans.

More Across Colorado

Herbed Salmon

salmon filet
olive oil spray
butter spray
4 tablespoons olive oil
¼ teaspoon *each* salt and dried basil
1 tablespoon dried mint leaves
1 teaspoon garlic (minced or powder)
¼ teaspoon lemon pepper
½ heaping teaspoon coarse ground pepper
¼ teaspoon *each* celery seed and dill
½ teaspoon onion powder
½ teaspoon Cajun seasoning
⅛ teaspoon turmeric
1 teaspoon dried chives
½ teaspoon orange zest
¼ teaspoon lemon zest
1 teaspoon lemon juice
2 tablespoons white wine, *or* white-wine
  vinegar
¼ teaspoon thyme, rubbed between palms
1 teaspoon Rose's sweetened lime juice

Cooking time: 20 minutes
Serves: 6 to 8

Place large piece of heavy-duty aluminum foil (large enough so sides can be folded to make a boat for salmon to lie in) on a cookie sheet.

Spray bottom of salmon with olive oil spray, then with butter spray.

Combine rest of ingredients into a marinade.

Apply a light coating of marinade on bottom of salmon.

Turn over and spray top of salmon with both olive oil and butter sprays.

Coat generously with remainder of marinade.

Place in boat.

Refrigerate for 30 minutes or more.

Grill the boat on low, 350° to 375° for about 20 minutes, or until salmon meat flakes, turning once during grilling.

Alternatively, bake at 350° about 20 minutes, or until meat flakes.

More Across Colorado

A pack train in the mountains.

LAKE CITY

From the mountain fastness of the San Juans, early settlers took a lively interest in current events. In the fall election of 1877, the question of the moment was whether Colorado women should be given the vote. Suffragist Susan B. Anthony toured the young state, urging Coloradans to vote yes. When she arrived in Lake City, so many packed the courthouse where she was to speak that she could not get to the rostrum. She delivered her speech outdoors, where the *Lake City Silver World* reported, "People stood for two hours in the cold night air and listened with rapt attention." Nevertheless, a few weeks later Lake City joined the rest of the state in voting against women's suffrage. Not until 1893 would the women of Colorado gain the right to vote.

More Across Colorado

Honey Baked Chicken

½ cup *each* butter and honey
¼ cup Dijon mustard
1½ teaspoons curry powder
4 boneless, skinless chicken breast halves,
    flattened to uniform thickness
¼ cup white raisins, optional

Cooking time: 1 hour and 15 minutes
Serves: 4

Preheat oven to 375°.
Melt butter in 9x13-inch baking dish.
Stir in honey, Dijon mustard and curry powder.
Roll chicken breasts in the honey mixture, coating well.
Arrange meaty side up in a single layer.
Bake at 375° for 1 hour and 15 minutes, or until chicken is tender and well glazed. Baste with honey mixture every 15 minutes.
If using raisins, sprinkle on top for last 15 minutes of baking time.

Luscious Onion Pot Roast

3 pounds beef chuck roast
4 medium potatoes, quartered
4 medium carrots, cut into 1½-inch pieces
2 stalks celery, cut into 1½-inch pieces
½ cup homemade Onion Soup Mix ➔
10¾-ounce can cream of mushroom soup

Cooking time: 2 to 3 hours
Serves: 6

Preheat oven to 325°. Cut 30x18-inch piece of heavy-duty foil, and place in 9x13fo-inch baking dish. Place roast in center of foil; arrange vegetables around roast, then sprinkle roast and vegetables with soup mix. Spoon mushroom soup over all.
Seal foil securely. Bake at 325° for 2 to 3 hours, or until tender.

Onion Soup Mix: Combine and mix well ¾ cup instant minced onion, ⅓ cup beef-flavor instant bouillon granules, 4 teaspoons onion powder, ¼ teaspoon celery seed, crushed. Yields 18 tablespoons (about 1 cup). Five tablespoons = 1.25-ounce package of store-bought mix.   Store in a cool, dry place in a tight-fitting container.

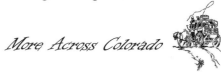

More Across Colorado

Treaties greatly reduced the size of Ute lands and created reservations for Ute settlement, such as this one at the Los Pinos Agency, c. 1868.

THE MOUNTAIN PEOPLE

This land once belonged to the Utes, "the mountain people," who hunted and lived here for generations. Their footpaths wound over the slopes and through the valleys. But in 1858, gold was found near present-day Denver, and the rush to the Rockies was on. No part of Colorado Territory, not even the San Juan stronghold of the Utes, was too distant or isolated for the fortune-hunting prospectors. Finally, white pressure led to the Brunôt Agreement of 1873, in which the Utes ceded the San Juans. As the snows melted the following spring, workers began building the first road into the area. Eager prospectors followed on the workers' heels, traveling down the road as it was cleared through the wilderness.

More Across Colorado

Mediterranean Chicken Wraps

This recipe may be refrigerated overnight. *

1¼ pounds boneless and skinless chicken
     breasts, cut into 1-inch strips
2 medium tomatoes, seeded and chopped
½ cup sweet onions, sliced
½ cup cucumber, seeded and chopped
2 tablespoons cider vinegar
1 tablespoon olive oil, *or* more to suit taste
1 teaspoon dried oregano
½ teaspoon dried mint, *or* basil
¼ teaspoon salt
3 whole-wheat pita breads, warmed, *or* 6
     tortilla-style wraps, warmed
6 lettuce leaves

Cooking time: 5 to 10 minutes
Serves: 6

In a large non-stick skillet, cook chicken for 5 minutes, or until no longer pink.
Remove from skillet; cool slightly.
In a bowl, combine the chicken, tomatoes, onion and cucumber.
Whisk together the vinegar, oil, herbs and salt.
Pour over chicken mixture; toss gently.
* *Cover and refrigerate for at least 1 hour, up to overnight.*

Line pita halves, *or* tortilla wraps, with lettuce leaves.
With slotted spoon, fill with chicken mixture.

More Across Colorado

Golden Fleece Mine

THE SILVER OF THE SAN JUANS

In the San Juan Mountains, it was long believed the gleaming metal - silver - could be found in abundance. Spanish explorers came in search of silver in 1765 and again in 1776. About a hundred years later, prospectors found both silver and gold. Lured by glowing articles in the *Lake City Silver World*, eastern investors soon built smelters and began operating the largest mines, the Golden Fleece and the Ute and Ulay. But by the mid-1880s, the high costs of hard-rock mining and the low grade of the ore forced many mines and smelters to close. Then came the collapse of the silver market in 1893 and an end to silver mining in the San Juans.

More Across Colorado

Pork Chop Casserole

4 boneless pork chops, ½-inch thick
garlic powder
1 can cream mushroom soup
4 red potatoes, peeled and sliced
salt
pepper
6 ounces butter, melted
½ large onion, chopped
2 cups shredded sharp cheddar

Cooking time: 1 hour
Serves: 4

Flatten chops with a mallet to about quarter-inch thickness.
Season pork with garlic powder and brown in a lightly greased skillet.
In a greased baking dish, layer soup, half of the meat, potatoes, salt, pepper, melted butter, onion, and repeat.
Top with cheese.
Cover with heavy foil.
Bake at 350° for 1 hour, or until potatoes are tender.

More Across Colorado

Antonito railroad depot, 1885.

THE CUMBRES & TOLTEC

Antonito grew out of the race to build the first railroad through the southern Rockies. The Denver & Rio Grande Western arrived in 1880, built the town, then kept pushing westward over a rugged, remote stretch of the San Juan Mountains. To save money and to accommodate the route's alarmingly tight curves, the D&RGW opted for narrow-gauge track. Clinging to the steep slopes as it twisted over the Continental Divide, the line reached Chama, New Mexico, in 1881, unlocking a vast region of timber stands, coal fields, and mineral veins. Later the railroad added deluxe tourist service, seating passengers in converted freight cars. Riders boarded at the old depot, which sits across the highway, to enjoy a day of scenic thrills.

More Across Colorado

Roast Pork with Fruit Sauce

3 to 4 pounds pork loin roast
1 cup apple juice
½ cup apple jelly
1 teaspoon ground cardamom
¾ cup dried cranberries, *or* other dried fruit(s)
    such as cherries, apricots, peaches

Cooking time: 1 hour to 1¼ hours
Serves: 6 to 8

Place roast in shallow roasting pan.
In a small saucepan, combine apple juice, jelly and cardamom.
Heat mixture until smooth, stirring frequently.
Pour over roast.
Bake at 375° for 1 hour to 1¼ hours, or until meat thermometer registers 160°. Baste every 30 minutes with jelly mixture.
Remove roast to cutting board; cover loosely with aluminum foil.
Transfer pan juices to a small saucepan; add cranberries, *or* other fruit(s); simmer 5 minutes or just until fruit is softened.
Slice roast and serve with fruit sauce.

More Across Colorado

Spinning wool, c. 1937.

WOVEN ACROSS TIME

The Hispano weaving tradition in the San Luis Valley reaches back to the sixteenth century when sheep were introduced to New Mexico. Through export and trade, Rio Grande blankets - those produced in New Mexico and in the San Luis Valley - soon achieved worldwide acclaim. Hispano textiles are not only functional but also beautiful and a source of family pride. One San Luis Valley weaver says of her work: "It's part of my soul. I want to be proud when I point to a piece and say, I made that!"

More Across Colorado

Shredded Beef

1 large rump roast
1 can beer

Cooking time: 8 to 10 hours

Place roast in crock pot and cover with beer.
Set pot on low and cook 8 to 10 hours.
Remove meat from broth.
Reserve broth and cool.
Allow meat to cool until it can be easily handled, but shred while still warm to the touch.
Divide into meal-sized portions.
Place in freezer containers.
Divide reserved broth evenly among containers.
Freeze until ready to use.

Note: Here are some serving suggestions.
- Drain broth and reserve before using meat. Add reserved broth as needed for your recipe.
- Heat meat with your favorite barbecue sauce and serve on buns.
- Heat meat with refried beans and make burritos. Add salsa and other ingredients your family enjoys.
- Brown onions, garlic and mushrooms with meat, and serve over noodles, rice or baked potatoes.

More Across Colorado

SAN LUIS

Working the San Luis People's Ditch. Courtesy San Luis Museum and Cultural Center.

Nearly every man, woman, and child in San Luis helped build the People's Ditch. Digging with makeshift wooden shovels and hoes, the pioneers carved the *acequia* in 1851 to transport water from the Culebra River. Because they lacked surveying equipment, they had to open the headgates as they worked to ensure that the channel flowed downhill. This community resource, the oldest recorded water right in the state, remains a focal point of life in San Luis. Every June 24, the town marks the opening of the canal with prayers and blessings honoring *San Juan Bautista* (Saint John the Baptist). Early celebrations featured children lining the banks to pluck toys and gifts from the surface of the water.

More Across Colorado

Sour Cream Enchiladas

This recipe calls for day-ahead preparation. *

12 corn tortillas
4 cups chicken, cooked and diced
2 10-ounce cans cream of chicken soup
4-ounce can diced green chiles
1 pint sour cream
1 pound cheddar cheese, shredded
1 small bunch green onions, including tops,
        chopped

Cooking time: 1 hour to 1½ hours
Serves: 8 to 10

Wrap tortillas in damp towel and warm in microwave oven until soft.

Combine chicken, soup, chiles and sour cream.

Place 2 tablespoons chicken mixture, 1 teaspoon cheese and 1 teaspoon green onion on each warm tortilla.

Roll tortilla; place seam-side down in greased 9x13x2-inch greased baking dish.

Roll all tortillas in same manner.

Spread remaining filling over top of rolled tortillas.

Sprinkle with remaining cheese.

Cover with foil.

* Let stand in refrigerator for 24 hours. Next day, bake at 350° for 1 hour to 1½ hours, or until bubbly.

More Across Colorado

ACEQUIAS

The *acequia* (ah-say-kya) system, a thriving example of environmentally wise self-government, merges influences from Spain and North Africa. *Acequias* are long, gently sloping ditches that carry water from rivers and streams to the fields. All users share responsibility for maintenance, and an elected *mayordomo* (superintendent) enforces the rules. Long, narrow land parcels run alongside the banks, guaranteeing all farmers equal access to water. Early settlers depended on cooperation and careful management to preserve this delicate ecological balance in this high, arid basin, and today's farmers still prefer this traditional system over modern irrigation methods. Costilla County's sixty-six active *acequias* continue to sustain productive harvests.

San Luis People's Ditch No. 1. Courtesy San Luis Museum and Cultural Center.

More Across Colorado

Southwestern Chicken

8 chicken breast halves, cooked and cubed
4 cups cooked white rice
2 cups sour cream
½ cup mayonnaise
6-ounce can diced green chiles
½ cup finely chopped green onions
1 pound shredded Monterey Jack cheese
¼ teaspoon garlic salt
8 ounces shredded cheddar cheese

Cooking time: 1 hour
Serves: 8 to 10

Combine all ingredients except the cheddar cheese.
Place in a greased baking dish.
Cover.
Bake at 350° for 30 minutes.
Uncover and bake for 25 minutes more, or until hot.
Sprinkle top with cheddar cheese.
Return to oven for 5 minutes, or until cheese is melted.

More Across Colorado

UNIVERSITY OF COLORADO

Although created by the territorial legislature in 1861, the University of Colorado did not open to students until 1877. That first year, only forty-four students were enrolled, ten of whom were classified as "preparatory." CU president Joseph Sewall, a Harvard M.D. and Ph.D., served as the university's only faculty member, teaching classes in natural philosophy, biology, botany, physics, chemistry, political economy, astronomy, physiology, and logic. Today, the University of Colorado is recognized for its excellence and spreads over campuses in Boulder, Denver, and Colorado Springs.

Old Main, University of Colorado, 1877.

More Across Colorado

Southwestern Chicken Pot Pie

double pie crust for 10-inch, deep-dish pie, homemade, *or* purchased

2 tablespoons butter

10¾-ounce condensed cream of chicken soup, such as Campbell's Creamy Chicken Verde Soup

½ cup half-and-half

½ cup sour cream

8-ounce can diced green chiles

½ cup favorite salsa

16-ounce bag frozen kernel corn, thawed

3 cups cubed cooked chicken

½ cup frozen southern-style, diced hash-brown potatoes

1 to 3 teaspoons ground cumin

1 to 3 teaspoons chili powder

1 tablespoon fresh, *or* dried, cilantro leaves – can substitute oregano

1 cup shredded Monterey Jack cheese

Cooking time: 45 minutes to 1 hour

Serves: 6 to 8

Preheat oven to 400°.

Place bottom crust in deep-dish pie plate. Do not prick crust.

Partially bake, 7 to 10 minutes.

Remove from oven; immediately press bubbles down with back of spoon.

Reduce oven temperature to 375°.

Combine butter with the next 5 ingredients, stirring well.

Stir in corn, chicken and potatoes, mixing well.

Add cumin, chili powder and cilantro.

Gently stir in shredded cheese.

Spoon mixture into pre-baked crust.

Top with second crust; seal edge, flute, and cut slits in several places.

Bake at 375° from 45 to 50 minutes or until crust is golden brown.

Let stand 10 minutes before cutting into wedges and serving.

More Across Colorado

TIMBER INDUSTRY

Frontier travelers often rejoiced upon reaching the timbered ridge just south of Franktown: The first woodland they encountered after hundreds of miles on the prairies. However, early settlers in Colorado appreciated the forest as a source of building material as well.. Known as the Pinery, it provided fast-growing Denver and other towns with most of their lumber during the 1860s. Several sawmills buzzed nonstop in and around Franktown, barely able to keep up with the demand. In the early 1870s, the Pinery supplied railroad ties to the Kansas Pacific and Denver & Rio Grande, both of which were laying tracks within twenty-five miles. Those routes eventually opened larger forests to exploitation and helped bring down this region's timber industry. By 1880, Franktown's sawmills had gone silent, but they had already left their mark: Pinery lumber built much of early Colorado.

Railroad construction gang, about 1870. Railroads required more than steel; they also required a large amount of lumber, especially for ties. Much of the lumber used by the Kansas Pacific and the Atchison, Topeka & Santa Fe railroads came from the forests surrounding Franktown.

More Across Colorado

Southwestern Pasta

1 tablespoon olive oil
½ cup chopped green onions
2 cloves garlic, minced
16-ounce jar salsa
8-ounce tomato sauce
1 cup whole kernel corn, fresh, *or* frozen
¾ cup canned black beans, rinsed and drained
½ teaspoon Cajun, *or* Southwestern seasoning
1 pound spaghetti, cooked and drained
1 pound boneless, skinless chicken breast
        halves
¼ cup jalapeño peppers, sliced, optional

Cooking time: 50 minutes
Serves: 8

Heat oil in a large non-stick skillet over medium heat.
Add onion and garlic, and sauté for 5 minutes.
Reduce heat to medium-low.
Stir in salsa and tomato sauce; cook 20 minutes, stirring occasionally.
Add corn, beans and seasoning; cook 4 minutes, *or* until thoroughly heated.
Keep warm.
Prepare grill or broiler.
Cook chicken for 5 minutes on each side or until done.
Slice chicken lengthwise into half-inch strips.
Spoon the sauce over pasta.
Top with grilled-chicken strips, and garnish with jalapeño peppers if desired.

More Across Colorado

In the early years of the timber industry, lumber suppliers primarily transported timber to mills via ox, mule, or - like this crew in the late nineteenth century - horse teams.

FRANKTOWN

Franktown takes its name from James Frank Gardner, a would-be gold miner who built a squatter's cabin in 1859. A popular rest stop on the busy Jimmy Camp Trail (which followed Cherry Creek into Denver), Frank's Town was designated the seat of Douglas County in 1861; the settlement moved to its current location two years later. Though railroads made the trail obsolete after 1870, and the county offices moved to Castle Rock in 1874, Franktown remained a ranching and farming hub, held together by its church, school, grange, and handful of businesses. It never incorporated, and during the twentieth century no more than a hundred people called it home, but that's how the locals liked it. Even as suburban sprawl surrounded it in the 1990s, Franktown resisted efforts to develop, maintaining a distinctly rural identity.

Spicy Beef Brisket

*This recipe needs to marinate from 12 to 24 hours. ** *

4 pounds beef brisket
2½ cups apple juice, *or* cider – use only a
　　quality product
½ cup soy sauce
¼ cup oil
2 bay leaves
1 clove garlic, chopped
1 large onion, chopped
½ teaspoon ground ginger
¼ teaspoon pepper
½ cup water
¼ cup cornstarch

Cooking time: 3 hours
Serves: 6 to 8

* Marinate the brisket in seasonings for 12 to 24 hours in large plastic bag.
Using all of the marinade, bake at 335° for 3 hours or until tender.
Discard the bay leaves.
Remove the brisket and let it rest for about 15 minutes before slicing.
Pour marinade into a small saucepan.
Mix the water and cornstarch and add to the marinade.
Cook and stir until thickened.
Serve marinade with thinly sliced brisket.

More Across Colorado

CHINESE IN COLORADO

Between 200 and 300 Chinese immigrants settled near Central City in the 1870s, forming the state's second-largest Chinese community (behind Denver). Most were former railroad construction workers who moved here in search of better prospects. But then, prospects for Chinese in the West were always limited by language barriers, discriminatory laws, and outright racism. Chinese mine workers in Central City earned lower wages than European immigrants did, and their only opportunities to mine for themselves were on leased claims that others had given up for dead. Yet they made those claims pay. This pattern repeated itself throughout the state: Chinese made the most of less-than-ideal circumstances, carving out livings as laborers, miners, and entrepreneurs - and doing much of the hard work involved in building Colorado. Though most of the early Chinese settlers eventually left, the descendants of those who remained welcomed new Chinese and other Asian immigrants to the state, particularly in the late twentieth century.

Chinese placer miners in the late 1800s. Although many of the Chinese in America came from farming or urban backgrounds, they became superior miners by working long hours, running tightly organized operations, improving existing tools, and working patiently to recover as much gold as possible.

More Across Colorado

Spicy Turkey Lasagna

1 pound ground turkey
1 teaspoon dried oregano
½ teaspoon salt
¼ to ½ teaspoon red pepper flakes
15-ounce container ricotta
2 cups shredded Italian blend cheese (8 ounces)
10-ounce package frozen chopped spinach,
    thawed and squeezed dry
12 lasagna noodles, uncooked and broken in
    half
26-ounce jar chunky pasta sauce with mush
    rooms and green peppers
½ cup water
grated Parmesan cheese, optional

Cooking time: 4½ hours
Serves: 8

In skillet, brown turkey over medium-high heat, breaking up clumps until no longer pink – 5 to 7 minutes.
Season with oregano, salt and pepper flakes.
Remove from heat.
In bowl, mix ricotta, blend cheese and spinach.
In oval slow-cooker, layer half the noodles, overlapping as necessary.
Spoon on half the meat mixture.
Pour on half the pasta sauce and half the water.
Then spread half the cheese mixture.
Repeat layering.
Cover slow-cooker and cook on low heat for 4½ hours.
To serve, cut into 8 equal pieces.
Sprinkle with Parmesan cheese, if desired.

More Across Colorado

CASTLEWOOD DAM

From the day it opened, Castlewood Dam was a catastrophe waiting to happen. Built in 1890 on Cherry Creek, the barrier stored enough water to irrigate 30,000 acres of farmland - or would have, if it hadn't leaked so badly. The seeping began the year the dam was completed and was serious enough that a hundred-foot section crumbled in 1897. Although its builders vouched for the structure's integrity, the dam continued to leak sporadically for decades. Finally, on August 3, 1933, the inevitable happened: Castlewood collapsed, sending a billion-gallon torrent toward Denver. Only two people drowned, thanks to a switchboard operator's life-saving calls, but the flood devastated farms in the area and tore out six bridges in Denver, thirty miles downstream. The dam's remains can still be visited in nearby Castlewood Canyon State Park.

Almost from the time workers completed construction, Castlewood Dam leaked. In 1901, farmers in the irrigation district that ostensibly benefited from the presence of the dam complained that there was not enough water in the reservoir to properly irrigate their crops.

More Across Colorado

Supreme Prime Rib Roast

Small-end, bone-in prime rib roast, any size
over 4 pounds

Au Jus paste:
½ teaspoon garlic powder
½ tablespoon paprika
2 teaspoons salt
1 tablespoon Accent, optional
¼ teaspoon cracked black pepper
2 tablespoons Worcestershire sauce
¼ cup solid shortening
1 bouillon cube, crumbled
1 teaspoon rosemary leaves, crushed

Cooking time: 2 hours plus
Serves: 8 to 10

Bring roast to room temperature.
Preheat oven to 375°.
Place roast in roaster pan, fat side up.
Mix together all Au Jus paste ingredients.
Spread over roast.
Bake 1¼ hours, uncovered. Turn off oven, leaving roast in.
Do not open oven door.
One hour before serving, turn oven to 300° and roast an additional
45 minutes.
Remove roast from pan and cover with foil.
Pour pan drippings into a saucepan.
Add 2 cups water and simmer.
Carve meat.
Pour Au Jus into a gravy boat and pass with meat.

Note: This is the traditional prime rib roast recipe, where the inside
is cooked medium-rare to rare, and the outside turns out done to
well-done. This recipe, from a country club in Iowa, is over 100
years old.

More Across Colorado

CHIN LIN SOU

Few Coloradans bridged the gap between Chinese and American culture as successfully as Chin Lin Sou. A native of southeastern China, he came to Colorado via California, arriving in 1870 to supervise construction crews for the Denver Pacific Railroad. After migrating to Central City to manage Chinese mine laborers, Chin began operating mines of his own (on claims leased from white owners), and he soon acquired interests in other mountain towns and in Denver. His success created many opportunities for the Chinese community, but Chin also reached across racial boundaries to forge friendships and ties with white businessmen. Although a federal law stripped him (and all Chinese) of U.S. citizenship in 1882, Chin remained an esteemed Colorado resident until his death in 1894. Marchers carried both the Chinese and U.S. flags in his funeral procession.

Chin Lin Sou (date of photograph unknown though probably in 1880s), an early Colorado settler and entrepreneur.

More Across Colorado

Sweet and Sour Brisket

This recipe requires overnight refrigeration. *

3 to 4 pounds beef brisket
15-ounce can sauerkraut, undrained
15-ounce can chopped tomatoes, undrained
1 cup brown sugar
½ cup water
¼ cup cornstarch
noodles

Cooking time: 4 to 5 hours
Serves: 8

Place brisket on aluminum foil in a roasting pan.
Cover meat with sauerkraut and tomatoes – do not drain either one.
Evenly distribute brown sugar over the top.
Seal foil and cook at 300° for 4 to 5 hours.
* Cool and refrigerate overnight. The following day, remove any fat and reheat.

To use liquid as gravy, pour into a small saucepan.
Mix the water and cornstarch and add to the liquid.
Cook and stir until thickened.
Slice the brisket and serve with noodles and the gravy.

More Across Colorado

Appliances like this electric range - available by the early 1910s - may not have removed all the drudgery from household chores, as some advertisers claimed, but they certainly required less labor than their coal-burning predecessors.

More Across Colorado

RURAL ELECTRIFICATION

Long after American cities were wired for electricity, many families in these remote prairies were still living by candlelight. The region's vast distances and meager customer base scared off big power companies. Even Hugo, which raised the funds to build its own electric plant in 1921, could not afford to stretch its service beyond the city limits. Nearby farmers and ranchers had to make do with improvised wind-powered generators, producing just enough voltage to run a sewing machine or a radio. In 1936 the Rural Electrification Administration finally began providing aid to unplugged areas, but while the paperwork pended and the grid was laid down, another generation grew up in the dark. The currents didn't flow to this countryside until 1951, making it one of the last parts of the nation to enter the electric age.

Yugoslavian Beef Stew - Djuvec

2 pounds boneless chuck steak, cut into 1½-
    inch cubes
2 tablespoons olive oil
2 tablespoons butter
2 tablespoons paprika
16-ounce can tomatoes
½ pound green beans, cut into ½-inch lengths
½ pound zucchini, cut into ½-inch-thick rounds
½ pound eggplant, peeled and cut into ½-inch
    cubes
10 peppercorns
10 garlic cloves
3 carrots, peeled and cut into ⅓-inch rounds
2 onions, chopped
1 bell pepper, chopped
2 bay leaves
1 tablespoon salt

Cooking time: 2¼ to 2¾ hours
Serves: 8

In a large oven-proof skillet, brown the meat in olive oil and butter.
Sprinkle with paprika.
Add remaining ingredients in layers.
Bring to a boil on top of the stove.
Cover skillet and bake at 350°.
Bake for 2 to 2½ hours, until meat is tender.

More Across Colorado

Between 1867 and 1880, John Hittson trailed several hundred thousand head of cattle from Texas to Colorado, and was instrumental in establishing Deer Trail as a railroad shipping point for cattle in 1870. Although not the only rancher in this region, Hittson certainly had one of the largest operations.

BEEF BONANZA

Like his fellow cattle kings, Tennessee-born John Hittson was an entrepreneurial marvel. From his Colorado headquarters northwest of Deer Trail, he marshalled disparate, far-flung resources to build a cattle empire four states wide. He overcame harsh weather and terrain, exploited free pasturage and the rise of the railroads, and lived like a feudal baron, the equal of Eastern industrial magnates. And why not? His operation was every bit as huge as theirs - and every bit as profitable. The cowboy may have caught the public's imagination, but it was men like Hittson who harnessed the land, water, labor, animals, and capital. They made the cattle business work, imposing order on a shapeless frontier.

Zucchini, Ham and Cheese Pie

1 large onion, sliced
3 zucchini, thinly sliced
1 large clove garlic, crushed
⅓ cup olive oil, *or* vegetable. oil
2 cups finely slivered ham
8 ounces sour cream (1 cup)
1¼ cups grated Swiss cheese
1 teaspoon dill weed
1 teaspoon salt – may be unnecessary
     depending on saltiness of ham
¼ teaspoon pepper
10-inch pie crust, unbaked
2 tablespoons butter
½ cup bread crumbs
¼ cup grated Parmesan cheese

Garnish:
tomato wedges
parsley

Cooking time: 45 minutes to 1 hour
Serves: 8

In oil, Sauté onion, zucchini and garlic.
Remove from heat.
Add ham, sour cream, Swiss cheese, dill weed, salt and pepper.
Mix thoroughly and spoon into unbaked pie shell.
Melt butter in small skillet; with a fork, stir in bread crumbs and Parmesan cheese.
Sprinkle mixture in a 2-inch band around pie edge, leaving middle open.
Bake at 350° for 45 minutes to 1 hour, until hot and bubbly.
Let stand 10 minutes before serving.
Garnish with tomato wedges and parsley.

More Across Colorado

The revenue from carrying airmail sustained early Colorado aviation. In 1926, pilot Floyd Pace (left) flew the Pueblo-to-Cheyenne, Wyoming, route.

FRONT RANGE FLIGHT

The Rocky Mountains proved a formidable barrier to early aviation, leaving Colorado in a familiar position: bypassed. As with the railroads fifty years earlier, transcontinental air traffic went through Wyoming; Colorado had to make do with a Denver-based spur line - in this case, Colorado Airways, which began flying the fifty-five-minute, Denver-to-Cheyenne route in 1926. Airplane technology quickly conquered the mountains, and Front Rangers began taking to the skies. In 1938, Continental Airlines became the state's first coast-to-coast passenger carrier, and after World War II Colorado became a major aviation hub, hosting Lowry Air Force Base and Buckley Naval Air Station as well as the U.S. Air Force Academy. Ultimately air travel changed life for Coloradans, tying them into national affairs as never before.

More Across Colorado

Apple Butter

8 cups unsweetened apple sauce
1 to 2 cups of sugar, depending on type of apple
    and its sweetness
4 teaspoons cinnamon
1 teaspoon allspice
½ teaspoon ginger
½ teaspoon cloves

Cooking time: about 3 hours
Yield: about six 8-ounce jelly jars

Place all ingredients in a shallow pan or roaster pan and mix well. Bake at 300° for about 3 hours, stirring every 10 to 15 minutes. Stir the apple butter away from the edge of the pan each time it is stirred.
This can also be cooked in a large pot on top of the stove, but the apple butter plops when it boils and splatters a lot.
Spoon into jelly jars and cap.
May be stored in refrigerator for several weeks, or sealed in canning jars using the hot-water bath method for about 5 minutes.

Blender Hollandaise

½ pound unsalted butter
6 egg yolks
4 to 6 tablespoons fresh lemon juice
½ teaspoon salt
¼ teaspoon freshly ground white pepper

Cooking time: 15 minutes
Yield: 1 cup

Melt butter until it begins to foam over medium-low heat – about 15 minutes. Meanwhile, place rest of ingredients into the jar of the blender. Cover and blend on high for 2 seconds.
With motor still running, gradually add melted butter in a slow, steady stream through the hole in the blender lid, leaving the milky solids behind. If sauce is too thick for your taste, just add a trickle of boiling water until it is the consistency that you desire.
Taste and adjust seasonings if necessary.

More Across Colorado

Denver Municipal Airport in 1931, soon after its first expansion - a second hangar.

Denver International Airport.

DENVER MUNICIPAL AIRPORT

Denver Municipal Airport opened in 1929, its four gravel runways squeezed onto a square-mile parcel in northeastern Denver. Boosters called it "the West's best airfield," but critics derided it as a pork-barrel reward for Mayor Benjamin Stapleton's political allies. Time proved out the boosters; by 1950 Stapleton Airport was serving six major airlines and 200,000 passengers, and in 1986 it ranked as the fifth-busiest airport in the world. Three years later voters authorized construction of Denver International Airport, a 34,000-acre facility to be supported by Front Range Airport and other satellite sites. Once again detractors cried boondoggle, particularly when construction glitches pushed the project behind schedule and over budget. When DIA finally went into service in February 1995, it was the largest airport in the world - and one of the most talked about.

Cherry Rhubarb Jam

6 cups rhubarb cut in 1-inch lengths
3 cups sugar
6-ounce package cherry or raspberry gelatin
21-ounce can cherry pie filling

Cooking time: 2 hours
Yield: 12 to 14 eight-ounce jars

Combine rhubarb and sugar in large pan, and let stand 1 hour to draw some juice from the rhubarb.
Cook mixture until rhubarb is tender – about 30 minutes.
Add gelatin and cherry pie filling and bring to a boil, stirring to dissolve gelatin and blend well.
Spoon into hot, sterilized jars; seal with canning lids.
Store in cool cupboard.

Cranberry Apricot Sauce

package whole cranberries, *or* 1 cup canned
    whole cranberry sauce
8-ounce package dried apricots, cut into small
    chunks
1¼ cups sugar for raw cranberries, *or* ¼ cup
    sugar for canned sauce
1½ cups orange juice
¼ cup water
1 or 2 tablespoons lemon juice

Cooking time: 35 to 40 minutes
Serves: 6

Combine all ingredients, then cook over medium heat until sugar dissolves.
Reduce heat and simmer for 30 minutes for raw cranberries, or less time for canned sauce.
Will thicken nicely.

Note: Serve warm with pork roast, turkey or salmon. Wild rice also goes well with this sauce.

More Across Colorado

In this late-1800s' rendition of the final minutes of the Reynolds gang at Russellville, southeast of Franktown, all but one of the troops fired over the heads of the gang members. Popular accounts portray the soldiers as having wanted no part of the execution ordered by Colonel John M. Chivington.

TERRITORIAL MILITARY ACTIVITIES

Franktown and Russellville both had small stockades in the early 1860s to protect this region from Confederate raiders, who hoped to tip the balance of the Civil War by gaining control of Colorado's gold fields. Manned by area residents (John Frank Gardner "commanded" the Franktown garrison), these local defenses supported Colorado's federal volunteer troops, who frequently patrolled the Jimmy Camp Trail. A group of volunteer cavalry camped near Russellville in 1863 while searching for Southern guerrillas, and six Texans (the infamous Reynolds gang) were executed there the following year. Territorial troops fought their most significant battle at Glorieta Pass in northern New Mexico, where the First Colorado Regiment helped turn back a sizable Confederate force in March 1862. Though far removed from the Civil War's main theaters, Colorado still had a hand in winning it.

Creamy Blue Cheese Dressing

32-ounce jar mayonnaise
1 pint coffee cream, *or* half-and-half
8 ounces Blue Cheese, crumbled
additional cream, optional
white pepper to taste

Mix mayonnaise and cream in mixer. Blend in blue cheese and white pepper. If you prefer a thinner dressing, blend in additional cream to reach desired consistency.
This is excellent for vegetable dips or for a large party.
Will keep refrigerated in quart jar for several weeks.

Story: This has been a family recipe for 30 years. *Marie Shaw*

Crock Pot Dressing

1 cup butter
2 cups *each* diced celery and diced onion
¼ cup parsley sprigs
2 8-ounce cans mushrooms, drained
12 to 13 cups slightly dry bread cubes
1 teaspoon poultry seasoning
1½ teaspoons *each* salt and sage
1 teaspoon thyme
½ teaspoon *each* pepper and marjoram
3½ to 4½ cups chicken broth
2 well-beaten eggs
turkey leg, *or* other uncooked poultry, optional

Melt butter in skillet and sauté celery, onion, parsley and mushrooms.
Pour over the bread cubes in a very large mixing bowl.
Add all seasonings and toss, mixing well.
Pour in enough broth to moisten.
Add eggs and mix well.
Pack lightly into slow cooker.
Set to high for 45 minutes; then reduce to low to cook 4 to 8 hours.
Optional: place chicken breast *or* turkey leg on top for added flavor.

Cooking time: 4 to 8 hours
Serves: 8 to 10

More Across Colorado

Laying the track.

More Across Colorado

TEN MILES A DAY

It is no coincidence that the West blossomed just after the Kansas Pacific Railroad's completion in 1870. The next generation witnessed the heyday of the cattle culture, which depended on Kansas Pacific railheads from Denver to Dodge City; the rush of prairie homesteaders, who shipped their produce to market in its boxcars; and the rise of industrial mines, whose ores rode the line to Eastern factories. Even as it helped construct a new frontier empire, the Kansas Pacific weakened the old one. The railroad ran through the heart of the Plains Indian nations, dividing their buffalo herds and expediting wars against them. As an economic pipeline and an engine of conquest, the Kansas Pacific played a central role in the transformation of the West.

August 15, 1870, was perhaps the greatest single day of railroad building in history. The Kansas Pacific tracks had surged to within fifty miles of Denver; a second crew, advancing eastward from the city, stood just over ten miles distant. At dawn on this day a U.S. flag and a keg of whiskey were placed halfway between the two crews, and the rhythmic calls of the gandy dancers commenced. By three in the afternoon the workers had bridged the gap; they laid ten miles of track in ten hours, a feat not matched before or since. Moreover, the Kansas Pacific made it possible to ride coast to coast without ever leaving the rails, while the Union Pacific still lacked a bridge over the Missouri River and required passengers to be ferried across at Omaha.

Easy Pie Crust

1 cup shortening
½ cup boiling water
2½ cups flour
¼ to ½ teaspoon salt

Yield: two 9-inch crusts

Pour boiling water over shortening.
Add flour and salt.
Stir until a ball forms.
Must be used while still hot or at least warm.
Proceed according to pie recipe being used

Great Pie Crust

If frozen, needs to be refrigerated for 24 hours before use. *

2½ cups all-purpose flour, plus more for work surface
1 teaspoon salt
1 teaspoon sugar
1 cup butter, chilled, cut into small pieces
¼ to ½ cup water

Cooking time: 10 to 15 minutes
Yield: two 9-inch crusts

Place four, salt and sugar in food processor and pulse to mix.
Add butter and blend until mixture resembles coarse meal – about 20 seconds.
Add ice water through the feed tube, mixing until dough holds together – about 30 seconds.
Turn dough out on work surface., halve and place each ball on a plastic sheet.
Flatten to form disk, cover in plastic and refrigerate for 1 hour.
Turn out on floured surface and roll out each disk to fit a 9-inch pie pan. Turn over as needed.
Bake at 450° for 10 to 15 minutes, or follow directions for fruit pie.
* Can be frozen for up to 1 month, but it needs to be moved to refrigerator 24 hours before rolling out.

More Across Colorado

PAY DIRT

Until 1859, gold existed mainly in rumor in Colorado, but it was a persistent rumor, dating back to the 1500s. Rumor became reality for thousands of doubters when, in a series of significant strikes beginning with George Jackson's discovery near present-day Idaho Springs in January, miners began to find bona fide lodes - not just sackfuls of dust, but vast fortunes. Though not the first strike, John Gregory's find between present-day Central City and Black Hawk in May brought thousands of miners up Clear Creek Canyon, miners who had begun to dismiss the rumor as a hoax. The Jackson and Gregory discoveries, among others, marked the beginning of the real Colorado Gold Rush, bringing tens of thousands of miners and settlers. John Gregory was not among them, however. Unsettled by fame and fortune, he sold his claim in 1862 for $21,000 and vanished from history. His lode eventually produced $200 million worth of gold.

Though John Gregory struck his mother lode in Clear Creek Canyon - the dream of every 59er - the fame he earned for his strike far exceeded his fortune.

More Across Colorado

Never Fail Pie Crust

4 cups flour
1 teaspoon each baking powder and salt
2 cups shortening
1 egg
½ cup water
1 teaspoon vinegar

Cooking time: 10 to 12 minutes
Yield: 3 pie crusts

Combine dry ingredients; cut in the shortening.
Beat the egg along with the water; add the vinegar.
Mix egg mixture into flour mixture.
Divide dough into 3 parts, pat into a disk, wrap in plastic.
Chill for 1 hour. Roll out on floured board.
Bake pie shell at 450° for 10 to 12 minutes.
If baking with a filling, follow recipe directions.

Gravy

8 large garlic cloves, chopped
¾ cup butter
1 tablespoon olive oil
1 bunch fresh parsley, leaves only
1 pound fresh mushrooms, sliced, optional
salt to taste
1½ cups flour
2 cups water
1 quart milk
¾ cup white wine, *or* chicken broth
salt to taste
a few drops Maggi seasoning, optional

In stock pot, fry the garlic in butter and olive oil till golden brown.
Add parsley and mushrooms, and continue to fry. Salt lightly.
In a separate bowl, whisk the flour and water until smooth. Add some of the milk to the flour mixture if it's too thick. Pour flour mixture in stock pot with the rest of the milk.
Add the wine, *or* chicken broth. Cook slowly so the gravy remains smooth. Stir occasionally until thickened. Salt to taste, and add Magi seasoning if you wish.

Cooking time: 30 minutes
Yield: 1½ to 2 quarts

More Across Colorado

SMELTING

Finding Colorado's gold was one thing; extracting it profitably was another problem entirely. Most of it was locked up in maddeningly complex ores, and there existed no efficient, cost-effective means of distilling out the pay-dirt. Not, that is, until 1867, when professor Nathaniel P. Hill perfected smelting. Adapting a Welsh ore treatment process, Hill used high heat and pressure to draw out the precious metals. His innovation threw open the West's mineral vaults and launched the era of industrial-scale, hard-rock mining; it also established Colorado as America's nineteenth-century ore-processing center. Mines throughout the West shipped their output to this area, first to Hill's Boston and Colorado Smelter (which opened at Black Hawk in 1868), later to massive refining complexes in Denver, Leadville, and Pueblo. Hill eventually became Colorado's third U.S. senator, and smelting emerged as one of the state's most important industries.

Nathaniel P. Hill surrounded by, clockwise, his wife, Alice, and their three children - Crawford, Isabel, and Gertrude - about 1876.

More Across Colorado

Homemade Frothy Eggnog

6 eggs, separated
1 pint whipping cream
14-ounce can sweetened condensed milk
1 quart milk
nutmeg as desired

Serves: 8 to 10

Beat egg whites stiff.
Fold in egg yolks.
In separate bowl, beat whipping cream stiff.
Fold whipping cream into egg mixture about one-third at a time.
Mix sweetened condensed milk with the milk until well blended.
Gently fold into egg mixture about one-third at a time.
Chill thoroughly.
Serve with nutmeg sprinkled on top.

Jalapeño White Sauce

2 cups whipping cream
1 cup sour cream
1 teaspoon chicken base
1 teaspoon juice from bottled jalapeños
1 teaspoon flour
2 teaspoons clarified butter
1 pound equal parts shredded jack and cheddar
        cheeses
1 jalapeño pepper, minced – can use fresh or
        bottled

Cooking time: 20 to 30 minutes
Yield: 3½ cups

Heat whipping cream over high heat until just before boiling.
Add sour cream and stir until dissolved, heating thoroughly.
Stir in chicken base and jalapeño juice and simmer.
Make a roux out of the flour and butter.
Just before the cream mixture boils again, add roux.
Mix well until smooth.
Remove from heat and stir in cheeses and minced jalapeño.

Note: This sauce can be used as a dip served with corn chips, *or* as a sauce with your favorite Mexican dishes.

More Across Colorado

TRAPPER'S TRAIL

Your journey along I-25 between present-day Pueblo and Greeley follows a centuries-old trail. Native peoples, Spanish and French explorers, American trappers, they all used it at various times. By the 1840s, most westerners knew it as the Trappers' Trail, named for the storied Mountain Men who trapped in this region from the 1820s and moved frequently between Bent's Old Fort on the Arkansas River to fur posts on the South Platte.

Thomas "Broken Hand" Fitzpatrick (1790-1854).

More Across Colorado

Baked Wild Rice

1½ cups wild rice
3 cups water
¼ cup vegetable oil
3 tablespoons soy sauce
1 large onion, chopped
1 cup chopped celery
12-ounce can mushrooms, including stems,
        pieces and liquid
1 envelope onion, *or* onion mushroom, soup

Combine all ingredients.
Pour into a 9x13-inch baking dish.
Cover with aluminum foil *or* lid.
Bake at 350° for about 2½ hours, until most of the liquid is absorbed.
Stir halfway through baking.

Cooking time: 2½ hours
Serves: 6

Basil Pesto Pasta

1 pound pasta of your choice
1 cup chopped fresh basil leaves – wash and
        gently pat dry before chopping
1 to 3 cloves garlic, to taste
½ cup pine nuts, *or* walnuts
½ cup freshly grated Parmesan cheese
½ cup extra virgin olive oil
additional Parmesan cheese

Cooking time: 20 minutes
Serves: 6

In blender, combine basil, garlic, nuts and cheese.
Slowly add olive oil while blender is running.
Makes 1½ cups of pesto.
Serve at room temperature.
Cook pasta according to package instructions.
Toss room-temperature pesto with well-drained pasta.
Serve with additional Parmesan.

More Across Colorado

Jim Baker (1818-98).

Christopher "Kit" Carson (1809-68).

A BREED APART

They wandered the uncharted Rocky Mountains, they went in harm's way, and they captured the imagination of Americans, then and now. But the Mountain Men were neither so free nor so independent as their legend insists. They toiled at the end of a long economic chain that stretched from the icy beaver ponds of the Rockies to the uncertain fashion markets of New York and London. Then in the 1840s, the supply of beaver ran out, and hat fashion changed from fur to silk. Suddenly, the day of the Mountain Men was done. Kit Carson became a guide, Jim Baker a rancher, and Thomas Fitzpatrick an Indian agent. Others were unable to fit in, forever on the move, always on the fringe of society, misfits to the end.

More Across Colorado

Cilantro Pesto Pasta

This recipe can be frozen for up to 3 months. *

1 cup cilantro leaves
½ cup parsley leaves
½ cup freshly grated Parmesan cheese
½ cup olive oil
¼ teaspoon kosher salt
1 to 3 large cloves garlic, amount to taste
¼ cup pine nuts
1 pound pasta of your choice

Cooking time: 20 minutes
Serves: 6

Combine all ingredients except pasta in a food processor, and process until well blended.
Cover and chill for at least 1 hour, but use at room temperature.
* *Can freeze for up to 3 months.*

Cook pasta according to package instructions.
Toss room-temperature pesto with well-drained pasta.
Serve with additional Parmesan.

More Across Colorado

Though Glidden patented his barbed wire in 1873, it was not extensively used in this area of eastern Colorado until the early 1900s.

BARBED WIRE

It took more than ten years and one thousand attempts to devise a fence for the treeless prairies. The breakthrough - barbed wire - was as hard and spare as the terrain, and it *had* to be. Patented in 1873 by Illinois farmer Joseph Glidden, the cheap, durable material kept homesteaders' crops safe from the trampling hooves of roving cattle. Though some stockmen denounced the barriers as an affront to the law of the open range, others raised their own fences, marking off huge pastures for their herds. Within a decade, barbed wire had transformed the geography of the West, bringing a sense of boundary to an unfettered expanse. Along with the windmill and the six-shooter, it helped make a hostile land habitable.

More Across Colorado

Creamy Garden Spaghetti

½ pound fresh broccoli, broken into florets
1½ cups sliced zucchini
1 large carrot, sliced
1½ cups sliced mushrooms
1 tablespoon olive oil, *or* vegetable oil
8 ounces uncooked spaghetti
1 tablespoon butter
¼ cup chopped onion
3 garlic cloves, minced
2 tablespoons flour
2 teaspoons chicken bouillon granules
1 teaspoon dried thyme
2 cups milk
½ cup shredded Mozzarella
½ cup shredded Swiss cheese

Cooking time: 35 to 45 minutes
Serves: 4

In a large skillet, sauté broccoli, zucchini, carrot and mushrooms in oil until crisp-tender.
Remove from the heat and set aside.
Cook spaghetti according to package directions.
In another saucepan, sauté onion and garlic in butter until tender.
Stir in the flour, bouillon and thyme until blended.
Gradually add milk.
Bring to a boil; cook and stir for 2 minutes or until thickened.
Reduce heat to low; stir in cheeses until melted.
Add the vegetable mixture; heat through.
Drain spaghetti; toss with vegetable mixture.

More Across Colorado

SEDALIA

Pioneer rancher John Craig built his Round Corral in 1859 next to a well-traveled road along Plum Creek. Other settlers followed, and when the Denver & Rio Grande Railroad pushed through in 1871, most of these neighbors moved slightly north to the present townsite. Originally called Plum, it was officially re-named Sedalia in 1882 after the postmaster's Missouri hometown; it became an important logging hub, as timber from the forests to the west built much of Denver and Colorado Springs. Dairy farms, a coal mine, and a cigar factory also prospered in the area, but these enterprises declined along with railroading during the mid-twentieth century. Although a 1965 flood damaged the town, the stability of area farms and ranches helped Sedalia withstand the currents of change and prosper into the twenty-first century.

George Manhart's store (seen here in the 1880s) was a Sedalia institution, offering a wide array of merchandise as well as a place to gather for local news and gossip. By 1890, the store (now a substantial brick building) was heated by steam, lighted by its own electrical plant, and eventually boasted the town's first phone booth. Courtesy Barbara Machann Collection.

More Across Colorado

Fettuccine Alfredo

8 ounces noodles
boiling salted water
6 tablespoons butter
1½ cups heavy cream
1 cup (3 ounces) freshly grated Parmesan
salt and pepper to taste
nutmeg, optional

Cook noodles and drain.
Melt butter, add ½ cup of cream. Simmer until slightly thickened. Reduce heat, add noodles and toss. Add salt and pepper, ½ cup of the cheese, ½ cup of the cream and toss. Add remaining cheese and cream, toss. Sprinkle with nutmeg if desired. Serve immediately.

Cooking time: 12 to 18 minutes
Serves: 4

Fettuccine with Clam Sauce

4 tablespoons butter
3 cloves of garlic, minced
½ cup finely chopped sweet onions
1 can minced clams with liquid
½ cup clam juice
1 pint whipping cream
1 small box fettuccine
¾ cup Parmesan cheese
salt and pepper to taste

Cooking time: 30 minutes
Serves: 6

Melt butter and sauté garlic and onion.
Add clams with liquid and the juice.
Cook over medium heat to cook down.
Add the cream. Simmer until it starts to thicken a little.
Cook fettuccine according to package directions. **Do not rinse.**
Sprinkle with Parmesan and seasonings. Toss.

Note: You can use more garlic and Parmesan cheese, to your taste. You can also add clams. You can also add prosciutto and peas. Beautiful and delicious.

More Across Colorado

In the summer of 1914, three Arapahos guided members of the Colorado Mountain Club through the mountains of Rocky Mountain National Park. From left to right: Shep Husted, Sherman Sage, Gun Griswold, interpreter Tom Crispin, Oliver Toll, and David Hawkins.

More Across Colorado

THE ARAPAHO INDIANS

In the mid-nineteenth century the Arapaho Indians lived on the High Plains between the North Platte and Arkansas rivers. Unlike most other Plains peoples, they wintered near the mountains, in the Boulder Valley or along the foothills north to the Medicine Bow Mountains of Wyoming. When gold seekers arrived in 1858, the Arapahos sought accommodation with the newcomers. In the end, however, conflict came and the Arapahos were eventually forced from their Colorado homeland. Today, the Northern Arapahos are on the Wind River Reservation in Wyoming, while the Southern Arapahos live on former reservation lands in Oklahoma.

Arapaho place names

The Arapahos called Longs Peak and Mount Meeker the Two Guides; the Estes Park basin was The Circle. Trail Ridge they identified as the Child's Trail, because children traveling it often had to get off their horses and walk. Big Thompson River was Pipe River, a place where the Arapahos carved their stone pipes. Grand Lake was Big Lake, site of a battle between Arapahos and Utes.

Great Noodles

¼ pound butter
8 ounces cream cheese
8 ounces sour cream
6 tablespoons sugar
2 teaspoons vanilla extract
3 eggs, beaten
juice 1 large lemon
grated lemon rind 1 large lemon
8-ounce package thin egg noodles, cooked to
          package directions, and cooled
3 tablespoons sugar
1 teaspoon cinnamon
6 ounces toasted almond slivers, optional

Cooking time: 1 hour
Serves: 8 to10

Cream together butter and cream cheese.
Add sour cream, sugar and vanilla.
Mix well.
Add the beaten eggs along with lemon juice and rind.
Fold cooked noodles into the sauce and spoon into a greased baking dish.
Mix sugar, cinnamon and almonds, if desired; sprinkle over the top.
Bake at 350° for 1 hour.

More Across Colorado

On July 10, expedition artist Samuel Seymoor sketched what were titled **Insulated Table Lands,** *today known as Larkspur Butte, Corner Mountain, and Nemrick Butte.*

More Across Colorado

LONG EXPEDITION, 1820

In 1820, Major Stephen H. Long trekked to the Rocky Mountains seeking the headwaters of the Platte, Arkansas, and Red rivers. When his 22-man party passed through the Larkspur area on July 9, the men marveled at the lush mountain scenery and spectacular landforms of the area. On July 12, the expedition paused near present-day Colorado Springs long enough for botanist Edwin James to scale Pikes Peak - declared "unclimbable" by Zebulon Pike only fourteen years before. Long never found the headwaters he sought, but the many species of plant life his expedition collected busied scientists for years, and his description of the Great Plains as a "Great American Desert" forever fixed itself upon the American mind.

According to a journal entry by Capt. John R. Bell of the Long Expedition on July 10, 1820, "A delightful discovery with our first entrance of what we may now call the Arkansas country - cool water from the mountain, numberless beaver dams and lodges. Naturalists find new inhabitants, the botanist is at a loss which new plant he will first take in hand - the geologist has grand subjects for speculation - the geographer and topographer all have subjects for observation."

Italian Rice

4 tablespoons fat
2 tablespoons chopped onions
2 tablespoons chopped green pepper
4 tablespoons chopped celery
3 cups cooked rice
¼ teaspoon paprika
2 cups tomatoes, chopped
½ teaspoon salt

Cooking time: 30 minutes
Serves: 4 to 6

In fat, brown onions, green pepper and celery.
Add rest of ingredients.
Mix well.
Pour into a greased baking dish.
Bake at 350° for 25 minutes.

Story: There is an old Denver story connected with this recipe, and it is told under **Apple Pudding** in **DESSERTS** - another recipe by the same cook.

Mexican Rice

¼ cup butter
1 cup chopped onion
4 cups cooked rice
2 cups sour cream
1 cup cream-style cottage cheese
½ teaspoon salt
3-ounce to 4-ounce can diced green chiles
2 cups grated cheddar cheese – more if desired

Cooking time: 45 minutes to 1 hour
Serves: 8

Preheat oven to 375°.
Lightly grease 9x13x2-inch baking dish (2 quarts).
Melt butter in skillet and sauté onion until golden brown – about 5 minutes. Combine all ingredients and pour into prepared dish.
Bake uncovered at 375° for 45 minutes to 1 hour, until hot and bubbly. If using additional cheese, after 50 minutes sprinkle the cheese on top and return dish to oven to melt cheese and finish cooking.

More Across Colorado

Faculty, University of Colorado, c. 1884.

BOULDER

British traveler Isabella Bird was not much impressed with Boulder City when she passed through it in 1873. "A hideous collection of frame houses on the burning plain," she described it. Founded by prospectors in February 1859, Boulder was a typical gold camp - here today, perhaps gone tomorrow. It escaped extinction by the discovery of silver in the late 1860s and by the Colorado territorial legislature's decision to make Boulder the home of the University of Colorado. With economic diversification and students and educators drawn from around the world, Boulder boomed and never looked back. Today, it is a famed educational and research center, and a major attraction for rock climbers and, despite Isabella Bird's bleak assessment, tourists.

More Across Colorado

Linguine alla Caprese

4 large ripe tomatoes, cut into ½-inch dice
½ cup fresh basil leaves, slivered
¼ cup fresh mint leaves, coarsely chopped
7 ounces ripe Brie with rind removed, torn into
      coarse pieces, *or* Mozzarella, cubed
2 teaspoons finely minced garlic
freshly ground black pepper, to taste
⅓ cup plus 1 tablespoon extra-virgin olive oil
12 ounces linguine, *or* spaghettini
salt, to taste
2 scallions – with 3 inches of green left on –
      thinly sliced

Cooking time: 15 to 25 minutes
Serves: 6

In a large serving bowl, combine the tomatoes, basil, mint, Brie, garlic, pepper and ⅓ cup of oil.
Bring a large pot of salted water to a boil. Add the remaining table-spoon of olive oil.
Add the pasta and cook until al dente – just tender, about 11 minutes.
Drain well, add the pasta to the tomato sauce and toss well; season with salt.
Garnish with the scallions.
Serve immediately.

Note: This quickly tossed, fresh tomato sauce can be made ahead and left at room temperature. Just before serving, cook the pasta, then toss it with the sauce, and garnish.

More Across Colorado

Despite their obvious advantages, steam tractors caused serious problems. Sparks emitted from the tractor's smokestack might set entire fields ablaze.

FROM HORSE TO TRACTOR

The settlement of eastern Colorado in the late 1800s coincided with a breakthrough in farming technology: the steam tractor. These remarkable devices could do the work of thirty horses, enabling tasks that once took weeks to be completed in days. Though too cumbersome and expensive for widespread use, they demonstrated the potential of mechanized agriculture and thus planted the seeds of progress. When gas-driven tractors appeared after 1900, they quickly uprooted the harness and plow. Farmers were able to keep fewer working animals on hand and tie up less of their acreage in pasture; they also saw less of their neighbors, as communal work patterns gave way to the impersonal labor of pistons and gears. But the transition brought clear gains in productivity and prosperity. By 1940, most Colorado farms were fully mechanized.

More Across Colorado

Pasta Famiglia Sola

¼ pound (1 stick) butter
8-ounce package cream cheese, *or* Mascarpone
1 teaspoon nutmeg
½ cup roasted and salted sunflower seeds
16-ounce package pasta – orecchiette, bowties,
    fusilli, rotelle, shells and the like
1 cup fresh parsley tips, very finely minced
Parmesan cheese if desired

Serves: 4 to 6

In wide and relatively shallow serving dish, cut butter and cheese into small pieces and allow to soften at room temperature. Once softened, cut in nutmeg and sunflower seeds, and set aside.

Cook the pasta in boiling, salted water for the time indicated on the package for pasta al dente. Drain thoroughly. **Do not rinse with cold water** as pasta must be as hot as possible when transferred to serving dish.

Gently mix pasta and sauce until all surfaces are coated. Sprinkle with minced parsley.

Serve hot.

Have Parmesan at hand in a separate bowl for those unfortunates who won't eat cheeseless pasta.

Note: This goes well with thin garlic grissini.

Story: This recipe comes from my North Italian family, where it was known as pasta al cavalleggero, or pasta cavalryman style. The name never made sense to me, but when I asked the cook once how one could possibly eat pasta while riding a horse, she glared at me in icy silence, and I never asked again. I've never found the recipe elsewhere, either. *Paulette Whitcomb*

More Across Colorado

Sterling, Colorado, 1936.

THE OVERLAND TRAIL

Call it the Pikes Peak Trail, the Denver Road, Overland Trail, South Platte River Trail - by any name, it dominated the movement of people and things in Colorado between 1858 and 1867, and it ranks with the great trails of American history. Travelers caught the pioneer highway at departure points along the Missouri River, then rolled along the Platte River through Nebraska to Julesburg, Colorado, where they turned to follow the river's South Fork to Denver only 180 miles distant. During its heyday, the road carried perhaps 166,000 people, fortune-seekers mostly, but merchants, settlers, and homesteaders, too. In 1866, however, the Union Pacific Railway chugged its way west to Julesburg, heralding the end of an era. By 1881, when new railheads such as Sterling greeted the great engine of settlement, the trail had become only a distant memory.

More Across Colorado

Penne alla Zucca

1 cup butternut squash, cut in large dice
1 cup acorn squash, cut in large dice
1 medium onion, diced
3 tablespoons olive oil
½ cup dry white wine
½ cup chicken broth, *or* vegetable broth
1 teaspoon dried sage, *or* 1 teaspoon fresh
    chopped sage
salt and pepper to taste
1 pound penne pasta
salt and pepper to taste
⅓ cup freshly grated Parmesan cheese
additional Parmesan, if desired
finely chopped parsley for garnish, if desired

Cooking time: 30 minutes
Serves: 4 to 6

Cook squashes in boiling water until pieces of each can be easily pierced with a fork, and then drain. Set aside.
Gently sauté onion in olive oil until translucent – not crisp.
Add wine and slowly reduce to concentrate flavors.
Add chicken, *or* vegetable, broth, squashes, sage, salt and pepper. Simmer.
Prepare penne pasta according to package directions – al dente is good.
Drain.
While pasta is still hot, toss with squash mixture.
Add salt and pepper to taste.
Season with Parmesan.
Serve with separate bowls of additional Parmesan cheese and parsley, if desired.

More Across Colorado

In a photograph taken near Sterling, a family poses in front of a sod house built about 1900.

STERLING

"Old" Sterling dates to the early 1870s, when displaced Southern families moved in and planted fields of wheat. Later, "new" Sterling flourished as a rail, ranching, and farming community. Here on the treeless High Plains, settlers found shelter in sod houses, universally and affectionately called soddies. One pioneer remembered: "The great thickness of the walls and their perfect joining with the earth itself provided a shelter so cozy and proof against the extremes of either heat or cold that [no one] who had once lived in one cared to abandon it completely."

Living in their earthen homes, these sodbusters created the great South Platte River farm belt, stretching from Denver to Julesburg, Sterling at its very heart. Though cattle were the mainstay of the region's economy, in the early 1900s sugar beets emerged as a major crop. Sterling's population boomed again in the 1950s when oil was discovered. From trail days to today, Sterling continues to play an important role in northeastern Colorado.

More Across Colorado

Polenta – Microwave

3 cups hot water
1 cup polenta meal, *or* corn meal
1 teaspoon salt
2 tablespoons butter
Parmesan

Cooking time: 15 minutes
Serves: 4 to 6

Combine all ingredients. Cover with plastic wrap, leaving one end open. Microwave 5 minutes on high.
Stir and repeat 3 times for a total of 15 minutes.
Serve with Italian red sauce, *or* brown gravy.
Sprinkle with cheese.

Story: I can remember my Italian grandfather standing at the coal cookstove making this dish for our family Sunday dinner. He used a wooden paddle to stir this dish for an hour or more. We adapted this recipe for the microwave and have this special treat for our Sunday dinner today. *JoAnn Simpleman*

Seasoned Rice Mix

3 cups uncooked, long-grain white rice
¼ cup dried parsley flakes
2 tablespoons instant chicken, *or* beef, flavor
        bouillon granules
2 teaspoons onion powder
½ teaspoon garlic powder
¼ teaspoon dried thyme leaves

Yield: 3 cups (4 servings)

Combine all ingredients and mix well.
Store in a cool, dry place in a tight-fitting container.
When ready to use, add 1 cup of this mix to 2 cups boiling water or broth and cook for 20 minutes or until desired texture.

Note: This economical, convenient mix can be used for poultry, fish or beef-flavored dishes. This mildly flavored side dish, using the homemade mix, offers great menu-planning flexibility at minimal cost.

More Across Colorado

Workers in sugar beet field.

ETHNIC SETTLEMENT

The first quarter of the twentieth century brought waves of immigrants to Brush. Many were Danish homesteaders, who staked claims throughout northeastern Colorado between 1870 and 1920. Another heavily represented population, Germans from Russia, known as the Volga Germans, came to work in Colorado's proliferating sugar beet fields after 1900. By the 1920s, Japanese men, Mexican Americans, and Mexican nationals had come here in force, lured by plentiful farm employment and the promise of better futures. Over time many of these newcomers became landowners themselves; others founded businesses or entered professions. The Japanese moved on, but the descendants of Danish, German, and Mexican immigrants have remained, making up a large and integral component of today's Brush population.

More Across Colorado

Risotto alla Milanese

Basic Risotto:
2 cups Arborio rice
7 to 8 cups chicken, *or* vegetable, stock
1 tablespoon minced garlic
½ medium-size white onion, finely diced
2 tablespoons olive oil
½ cup grated Parmesan cheese
salt and pepper to taste

Variations to basic risotto:

- Add 1 to 1½ cups cooked, chopped seafood, and heat through.
- Add 1 cup grilled asparagus, cut into 1-inch lengths.
- Add 2 tablespoons fresh squeezed lemon juice and ½ teaspoon grated lemon rind – especially good with grilled fish.
- Add 3 ounces of porcini mushrooms that have been soaked, drained, and roughly chopped or sliced.

Cooking time: 30 minutes
Serves: 4 to 6

Heat stock to boiling point.
In a heavy sauté or sauce pot, heat olive oil and sauté the onion until soft.
Add garlic and sauté.
Add rice and stir to coat.
Cook rice for 2 to 3 minutes, and then begin to add hot stock 1 cup at a time, stirring constantly.
When rice has absorbed most of the liquid, add the next cup.
Continue this until all the liquid has been absorbed, and the rice is creamy.
If you are going to do a variation, this is where you add those ingredients.
Add salt and pepper, to taste, and stir in Parmesan.
Serve immediately.

More Across Colorado

More Across Colorado

JARED L. BRUSH

Cattle pioneer Jared Brush never lived in the town named after him, but the community caught his enterprising spirit anyway. It produced one of the nation's first nursing homes, Eben-Ezer, which began in 1903 as a tuberculosis sanitarium, and then focused on its groundbreaking work in elder care during the 1920s. Local farmers thrived on sugar beets, dividing their crops between Brush's Great Western Sugar Company factory and area ranchers' feedlots. Oil drillers tapped the Little Beaver field in 1931; by the 1950s it was gushing nine thousand barrels a day. Brush later boasted Colorado's first pari-mutuel racetrack, a half-billion-dollar power plant, and a major meat-packing house; it remains a national leader in the care of the aged. Through it all, the town has remained one of the state's ranching meccas. Jared Brush would have been proud.

Jared L. Brush. The story goes that the town of Brush got its name when the telegraph operator at the local depot asked his superior what he should call "this place." The reply, "Why don't you name it for that fellow who ships all those cattle from there."

Artichoke-A-Roni

1 package chicken-flavored Rice-A-Roni
2 small jars marinated artichoke hearts, drained
    – **but reserve liquid**
2 green onions, minced
8 to 10 green olives, sliced
1 small can tiny shrimp, rinsed and well drained
½ red bell pepper, chopped

Prepare Rice-A-Roni according to package directions and chill thoroughly.
Cut artichoke hearts into quarters, combine with remaining ingredients. If too dry, add reserved artichoke liquid.
Blend rice and artichoke mixture.
Chill well before serving.

Cooking time: 20 minutes
Serves: 8 to 10

Asparagus Leek Soup

2 tablespoons unsalted butter
3 medium leeks, white part only, cleaned and
    chopped
2 garlic cloves, minced
4 14.5-ounce cans chicken broth
2 bunches asparagus, trimmed and cut in 1-inch
    pieces
½ cup heavy cream, *or* plain low-fat yogurt
salt and pepper to taste
minced chives for garnish

Heat butter in large pot over medium heat.
Add leeks and garlic; sauté until softened, 5 to 7 minutes.
Add chicken broth and asparagus and bring to boil; reduce heat and simmer 12 to 15 minutes.
With hand-held immersion blender, purée until smooth, *or* purée in a blender. If using a blender, do not fill more than one-third full and make certain that you partially open its top for heat ventilation – *or* place a small funnel in the hole in the lid to prevent splattering.
Stir in cream *or* yogurt.
Season with salt and pepper; garnish with minced chives.

Cooking time: 30 to 40 minutes
Serves: 8

More Across Colorado

Checking out the stock.

GOING, GOING, GONE ...

The cattle industry and the history of Brush have always been linked. The Burlington Railroad founded it in 1882 where the tracks intersected the Texas-Montana cattle trail; old-timers spoke of streets so choked with livestock that children couldn't walk to school. Though the great drives ended in the 1890s, Brush remained northeastern Colorado's most important railhead, becoming one of only two cattle stops on the California-Chicago route. The Brush Auction and Livestock Exchange opened in 1937 and before long was moving 120,000 head per year, making it one of the busiest locales in the U.S. cattle trade. Steers no longer roam the streets, but Brush's cow-town spirit is as strong as ever: The town's annual July 4 open rodeo is the largest contest of its type in the nation.

More Across Colorado

Bacon, Lettuce and Tomato Salad with Chicken

Dressing:
½ cup mayonnaise
4 tablespoons barbecue sauce
2 tablespoons finely chopped onion
1 tablespoon lemon juice
¼ teaspoon pepper

Salad:
10 cups romaine lettuce, torn
2 large tomatoes, seeded and diced
1½ pounds chopped, cooked chicken breast
10 strips bacon, cooked crisp and crumbled
2 hard-boiled eggs, sliced

Cooking time: 20 minutes
Serves: 8

Dressing:
Combine the ingredients in a small bowl; mix well.
Cover and refrigerate until serving.

Salad:
Place the salad greens on a large serving platter.
Sprinkle with the tomatoes, chicken and bacon.
Garnish with the eggs.
Drizzle with the dressing.

More Across Colorado

Great Western Sugar Factory, Fort Morgan c. 1915. Originally, the factory could process 600 tons of beets a day; today it processes 6,000. Today's grower-owned Western Sugar Cooperative factories process more than 24,000 tons daily.

GREAT WESTERN SUGAR

For more than half a century, the Great Western Sugar Company helped drive the economy of Colorado's eastern prairies. The conglomerate built fifteen processing plants along the South Platte and Arkansas Rivers between 1901 and 1910, creating economic opportunity for local farmers, laborers, packers, shippers, and sundry other agents. Towns competed vigorously to attract Great Western mills, and no wonder: After Fort Morgan's factory opened in 1906, the city's land values soared from $40 to $250 per acre. Great Western prospered into the 1970s, but corporate neglect caused a steep decline; one by one its plants shut down, leaving only Greeley and Fort Morgan operating. 1986 saw new ownership and a new name, Western Sugar. In 2002, the company became the grower-owned Western Sugar Cooperative; as such, it returns all its income to the local community. Headquartered in Denver, the cooperative has 135,000 acres under sugar beet cultivation in Colorado and three other Western states.

More Across Colorado

Broccoli Salad

This recipe may be refrigerated overnight. *

4 cups finely chopped broccoli, *or* 2 cups
    broccoli and 2 cups cauliflower
½ cup chopped red onion
1 cup raisins, *or* Craisins
2 tablespoons white vinegar, *or* rice vinegar
¼ cup sugar
1 cup mayonnaise
½ cup sunflower seeds
8 slices crisp bacon, crumbled

Toss the vegetables and raisins, *or* craisins, with a dressing of the next 3 ingredients.

* *Refrigerate 3 hours to overnight before serving.*

Just before serving, top with the sunflower seeds and bacon.

Serves: 6

Cajun Chicken Tortilla Soup

1 package Mahatma Red Beans & Rice
2 14.5-ounce cans diced tomatoes, undrained,
    or Mexican diced tomatoes seasoned
    with lime juice and cilantro
3 cups chicken broth
3 to 4 chicken breast halves, cooked and diced,
    seasoned with 2 teaspoons chili powder
8 ounces Monterey Jack with jalapeños,
    shredded
tortilla chips, broken

Prepare beans and rice according to package directions.
Combine diced tomatoes and chicken broth in large saucepan.
Bring to a boil.
Add cooked chicken, and reduce heat; cook for 7 minutes.
Add prepared bean-rice mixture; heat through.
Spoon into bowls.
Top with shredded cheese and broken tortilla chips.

Cooking time: 7 minutes

More Across Colorado

FORT MORGAN

Fort Morgan, 1908. The city was named for Col. Christopher Morgan, a Civil War hero, a man who never came west of the Mississippi.

Junction Station, the first settlement at this site, suffered numerous Indian attacks similar to those that raged all along the South Platte during the mid-1860s. To protect the crucial crossroads, which joined the South Platte River Trail with its Denver cutoff, the U.S. Army established Camp Junction in 1864. In 1866 Fort Morgan, roughly the size of a city block, was completed. The post defended the Trail, but traffic soon shifted north to the transcontinental rail corridor, and Fort Morgan was abandoned in 1868. Sixteen years later Abner S. Baker founded the present-day town and named it after the old battle station. Today one of eastern Colorado's most important cities, Fort Morgan has anchored life on the plains for more than a century.

More Across Colorado

Brown Rice Salad

Salad:

3 cups cooked brown rice

3 cups boned and skinned chicken breast
　　　halves, grilled and cubed

2 medium-size Granny Smith apples, diced

1 medium-size sweet red pepper, seeded and
　　　diced

2 celery ribs, finely chopped

⅔ cup green onions. sliced

½ cup chopped pecans, optionally toasted

Dressing:

¼ cup cider vinegar

3 tablespoons olive oil

1 tablespoon lemon juice, optional as dressing
　　　may become too sour

1 teaspoon salt

¼ teaspoon pepper

Cooking time: 40 minutes

Serves: 8

In a large bowl, combine the salad ingredients.

In a jar with a tight-fitting lid, combine the dressing ingredients.
Shake well.

Pour the dressing over the rice mixture and toss to coat.

Serve immediately, *or* refrigerate.

More Across Colorado

JOHN WESLEY ILIFF (1831 - 1878)

John Wesley Iliff ran the first large stock-growing operation in Colorado and the greater West. A native of Ohio, he had come to Colorado with the Gold Rush of 1859, but soon ranged his cattle on ranches and line camps that stretched more than a hundred miles through northeastern Colorado. Near Grover, he ran cattle on holdings scattered along Crow Creek and its tributaries. Like the cowboys he hired, Iliff roamed across the range and slept under the open sky. But unlike other ranchers, he rarely found it necessary to carry a weapon, perhaps because he made it known to the Indians that they were welcome to any cattle they needed. At his death, his estate was valued at more than $1 million.

John W. Iliff

More Across Colorado

Chinese Spinach Salad

Salad:
1 pound spinach, washed and torn
4 ounces water chestnuts, sliced and rinsed
1 package fresh bean sprouts, approximately
　　　　1½ cups

Dressing:
1 cup salad oil
¼ cup cider vinegar
⅓ cup ketchup
⅔ cup sugar
1 medium onion, chopped
salt to taste

Garnish:
2 hard-boiled eggs, cooled and mashed
6 slices crisp bacon, crumbled
1 can mandarin oranges, well drained
¼ cup sliced almonds, toasted

Serves: 8

Toss together spinach, water chestnuts and bean sprouts. Refrigerate until ready to serve.

Dressing:
Shake all ingredients together in a jar or plastic container. Toss salad with dressing.

Garnish:
 Place eggs, bacon, oranges and almonds across the top.

More Across Colorado

Family posing in front of soddy.

SETTLING THE GRASSLANDS

The towns of Raymer and nearby Stoneham began in the optimism of the 1880s with the homesteaders pouring onto the plains to "take up the land." Both towns were platted in 1888. Soon they boasted general stores, lumberyards, banks, livery stables, and hotels. Houses were often soddies and dugouts built from the earth, the cheapest and most available material. But the cycle of harsh winters and summer drought during the 1890s drove many homesteaders from the land. Town businesses closed, and people moved away. A new century brought new settlers, however, and New Raymer and Stoneham sprang to life again. Today, they are still the social and supply centers for surrounding farms and ranches.

Cold Avocado Soup

1 can chicken broth
1 to 2 avocados, peeled and cut in large chunks
1 teaspoon salt
½ teaspoon pepper
hot pepper sauce, to taste
juice of 1 lime

Serves: 4

Place all ingredients in the blender and process until smooth. Chill well before serving.

Cool Green Fruit Salad

3-ounce package lime gelatin
1 cup boiling water
1 cup vanilla ice cream
1 cup cottage cheese
1 cup crushed pineapple
2 maraschino cherries, rinsed and dried, cut in
    half, for garnish
whipped topping, optional

Serves: 6 to 8

In a 9-inch square dish, pour the lime gelatin and boiling water.
Stir, scraping the bottom until all the gelatin is dissolved.
While still hot, add the ice cream and stir until it melts.
Add the cottage cheese and pineapple.
Refrigerate.
After gelatin has set, place cherries on top for color.
If using whipped topping, spread on gelatin and place cherries on top.

More Across Colorado

EVANS

Bands played and banners flew when the first Denver Pacific Railroad engine steamed into Evans in December 1869. The town had good reason to celebrate: As the railroad's endpoint (and, at that time, the closest depot to Denver), it became Colorado's main transportation hub, the very center of the action. But the party ended abruptly the following spring, when the railroad bridged the South Platte and headed toward Denver, taking most of the commercial activity with it. Evans stood nearly empty until the following summer, when the St. Louis-Western Colony brought 400 settlers to the area. For the next several decades, Evans made a steady living as an agricultural supply town and highway service stop; when the Front Range suburbs expanded dramatically in the late twentieth century, the town became more residential without sacrificing its rural character.

Though he made his fortune in business, John Evans originally trained as a physician. Before moving west in 1862, Evans co-founded Northwestern University and developed the suburb of Evanston, Illinois.

More Across Colorado

Confetti Salad

This recipe may be refrigerated overnight. *

Salad:
10-ounce package frozen petite peas, steamed 5
    to 6 minutes, *or* 2 cans LeSueur Peas
1 can French-style green beans, drained, *or* 1
    cup frozen
1 can shoe peg corn, drained, *or* small-kernel
    frozen white corn
1 cup onions, chopped or sliced
1 cup diced celery
1 cup chopped, red bell pepper

Dressing:
½ cup oil
¾ cup vinegar
1 cup sugar, *or* ½ cup sugar substitute
lemon pepper to taste, optional
seasoned salt to taste, optional
garlic powder to taste

Serves: 4

Drain and combine peas, beans and corn. Add onions, celery and red pepper.
Whisk dressing ingredients together until sugar is well incorporated.
Pour dressing over vegetables.
* *Marinate at least 6 hours **or** overnight in refrigerator.*

More Across Colorado

FORT VASQUEZ

Andrew W. Sublette

As trappers and explorers, Louis Vasquez and Andrew Sublette helped build the lucrative fur trade. But by 1835, when they raised Fort Vasquez midway between Fort Laramie and Bent's Old Fort along Trapper's Trail and went into business for themselves, the fur industry was nearly played out. Three nearby forts competed for dwindling trade, and the two veteran Mountain Men, unable to turn a profit, sold the post in 1841 for just $800. Failing to collect even that sum, the new owners went bankrupt and abandoned the place in 1842. In later years a series of tenants - U.S. Cavalry units, stagecoach operators, and mail riders - occupied the structure for short periods, but after the 1860s the only visitors to Fort Vasquez were curious homesteaders and tourists.

More Across Colorado

Cranberry Salad

2 cups raw cranberries
1½ cups water
1 cup sugar
1 small package cherry gelatin
½ cup crushed pineapple, including juice
1 tart apple, peeled and chopped
½ cup chopped walnuts, optional

Cooking time: 20 minutes
Serves: 8

Add water to cranberries, bring to a boil, reduce heat, and simmer for 10 minutes. They will start to burst and mixture will thicken. Gradually add the sugar and stir over low heat until it dissolves. Remove from heat, stir in the gelatin, and continue to stir until it dissolves. Cool.
Sir in fruits and nuts. Pour into a mold and refrigerate until set. Remove from mold and serve.

Story: This recipe was a favorite of my mother's, Mrs. Sam Barnes of Vermillion, Kansas, and it has been a favorite of our family and friends for over half a century. We especially enjoy it at holiday time. *Winifred Modica*

Creamy Onion Soup

2 cups thinly sliced onions
½ cup butter
¼ cup flour
2 cups chicken broth
2 cups milk
2 cups (8 ounces) shredded Mozzarella

Cooking time: 20 to 30 minutes
Serves: 6

In saucepan over medium-high heat, cook onions in butter until tender – 7 to 10 minutes.
Stir in flour until well blended; gradually add broth and milk.
Bring to a low boil over medium heat, stirring constantly.
Cook and stir for about 1 minute.
Reduce heat to low, and stir in the cheese.
Stir and cook until cheese is just melted. ***Do not boil.***

More Across Colorado

PLATTEVILLE

Louis Vasquez

In the 1930s, the New Deal's Works Progress Administration rebuilt the crumbling outer walls of Fort Vasquez. Three decades later, the Colorado Historical Society launched an archaeological study to reconstruct daily life inside the complex. Painstaking excavations revealed roughly a dozen rooms around a large interior plaza. Visiting traders kept their pack animals in wooden stalls along the east wall, cooked and dined in a communal kitchen, warmed themselves beside brick fireplaces, and conducted business in large trading rooms. Storage chambers, a smithy, and the two proprietors' living quarters completed the fort. The rubble of the old fort yielded a wealth of buttons and beads, the currency of the fur trade - long-lost funds from forgotten transactions.

More Across Colorado

Creamy Tomato Rice Soup

1 onion, chopped
1 to 2 cups finely chopped celery
1 teaspoon minced garlic
¼ cup butter
4 large tomatoes, chopped
2 10.5-ounce cans tomato soup
2 cups half-and-half
2 cups cooked rice
1 tablespoon chopped fresh basil, *or* dill
salt and pepper to taste
water, optional

Cooking time: 20 minutes
Serves: 6 to 8

Sauté onion, celery and garlic in butter until soft.
Add the tomatoes.
Cook several minutes.
Add the tomato soup, half-and-half and cooked rice.
Heat thoroughly but ***do not let boil.***
Add seasonings.
If a thinner soup is preferred, add up to 2 soup cans of water.

More Across Colorado

Battle of Beecher Island, *Robert Lindneux, 1926.*

BATTLE OF BEECHER ISLAND

In September 1868, fifty civilian scouts left Fort Wallace, Kansas, to fight Cheyenne and Sioux warriors, on the theory that experienced frontiersmen could defeat any enemy force. On September 17, the scouts approached the Arickaree River, where Indians attacked them. Retreating to a sandbar, the command held off repeated charges for four days. In the fierce combat, the besieged unit suffered eighteen wounded and five men killed, including Lt. Frederick H. Beecher. The great Cheyenne war leader Roman Nose fell on the first day, but otherwise Indian losses were minimal. On September 25, the Tenth Cavalry - the famed African-American Buffalo Soldiers - rode to the scouts' relief. The frontiersmen had battled heroically, but never again did the Army send an independent civilian command to fight Indians.

More Across Colorado

Cumin Bean Salad

Salad:
4 cups chopped tomatoes
15-ounce can garbanzo beans, rinsed and
  drained
15-ounce can black beans, rinsed and drained
15-ounce can dark red kidney beans, rinsed
  and drained
1½ cups chopped red onion
1 cup minced fresh cilantro

Dressing:
¼ cup lime juice
½ cup extra-virgin olive oil
2 teaspoons chili powder
3 teaspoons cumin
1 teaspoon salt
½ teaspoon pepper

Serves: 10-12

In large bowl, combine tomatoes, beans, onion and cilantro.
In jar with tight-fitting lid, combine remaining ingredients; shake well.
Pour dressing over the salad and toss until well coated.
Refrigerate at least 4 hours before serving.

Note: In the summertime, add cooked chopped chicken breast for a main-course meal along with garlic bread – it's wonderful on a hot day.

More Across Colorado

BATTLE OF SUMMIT SPRINGS

JULY 11, 1869

At Summit Springs, the Fifth U.S. Cavalry, commanded by Maj. E. A. Carr, and a force of Pawnee Scouts attacked Chief Tall Bull's Cheyenne Dog Soldier village. Also prominent in the fight were chief of scouts William F. "Buffalo Bill" Cody, and the famed North brothers - Major Frank North and Captain Luther North. When the fighting was over, fifty-two Cheyennes lay dead. The Battle of Summit Springs - a great victory for the Army - broke the military power of the Dog Soldiers and ended Indian-white conflict on Colorado's eastern plains. Shortly after the battle the United States removed the Southern Cheyennes to reservation lands in present-day west-central Oklahoma.

William F. "Buffalo Bill" Cody c. 1867.

More Across Colorado

Dilly Potato Salad

*This recipe gains from marinating in refrigerator overnight. ***

2 pounds small red potatoes, scrubbed
½ large white onion
½ cup bottled Italian salad dressing – can be
      fat-free
¼ cup olive oil
salt and pepper to taste
1 cup chopped celery
4 hard-boiled eggs, chopped
¼ cup sliced pimento-stuffed green olives
⅔ to 1 cup mayonnaise, to taste
4 tablespoons fresh dill, *or* 2 tablespoons dried
      dill

Cooking time: 45 minutes
Serves: 8 to 10

Boil potatoes until tender when pierced with a fork.
Plunge potatoes into cold water and let cool for a few minutes, until they can be handled.
Slice potatoes, leaving jackets on, into a deep bowl.
Slice onion paper-thin, and then chop.
Add onion to potatoes.
Add salad dressing, olive oil, salt and pepper.
* *Toss, cover the bowl and marinate in the refrigerator overnight,* **or** *for a minimum of 4 hours.*

Just before serving, add the remaining ingredients, and mix well.

More Across Colorado

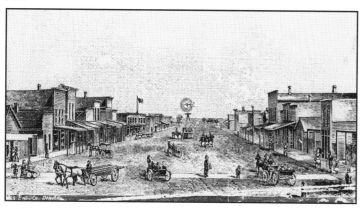

Akron, 1888.

AKRON

The Lincoln Land Company, a division of the Chicago, Burlington, and Quincy Railroad, thought a likely site for a new town was the highest point between Chicago and Denver. And Akron, the Greek word for summit, seemed an appropriate name for a railroad division station. So it was done. Platted in 1882 and incorporated in 1887, Akron developed as a railroad, farming, and ranching hub. Through dry and rainy cycles, and a few tornadoes, too, the town thrived, growing beyond its railroad origins. In 1907, the U.S. Department of Agriculture created an experimental station a few miles east of town; and, since 1952, a range cattle station examines grassland conservation. In the 1990s, Akron's great airport - featuring a 7,000-foot-long, 100-foot-wide runway, 24-hour weather station, and signal beacon used by pilots to chart cross-country courses - makes Akron a crossroads of the nation's interstate air carriers.

More Across Colorado

Fruit Salad

15½-ounce can chunk pineapple, drained
11-ounce can mandarin oranges, drained
20-ounce package frozen strawberries, thawed,
    or 1 pint fresh
4 bananas, peeled and sliced
21-ounce can peach pie filling

In large bowl, mix all fruit together.
Pour pie filling over the fruit.
Gently stir until fruit is well covered.
Chill well before serving.

Serves: 6 to 8

Greek Artichoke Salad

1 cup extra-virgin olive oil
1 small jar marinated artichokes, drained but
    reserving 1 tablespoon liquid
1 small can anchovies in oil, mashed, optional
freshly ground pepper to taste
1 clove garlic, minced
7-ounce, *or* 8-ounce jar pitted green olives,
    drained
1 large can pitted ripe olives, drained
15-ounce can garbanzo beans, rinsed and
    drained
1 large head romaine lettuce torn into bite-size
    pieces
1 package onion garlic croutons

Stir together oil, artichokes, artichoke liquid, anchovies if using, pepper and garlic.
Cover and marinate 4 to 6 hours.
When ready to serve, add olives and garbanzo beans to marinated mixture.
Mix well.
Toss with romaine lettuce.
Serve with croutons on top.

Serves: 6 to 8

More Across Colorado

GROVER

Grover was platted in 1889 as a way station on the Burlington and Missouri River Railroad, known locally as the Prairie Dog. Trains whistling across the plains stopped here to load cattle from nearby ranches. A two-story wood depot was built, and then stockyards. Soon hotels, stores, lumber yards, livery stables, and houses began to spring up. The first postmaster named the town Grover, his wife's maiden name. Over the years, Grover remained a commercial and social center for the surrounding farms and ranches. There was always reason to go to town: Dances at the depot or school, box suppers, pie socials, picnics. "Life on the homestead was lonely," said one rancher. "Once each month a time was set aside for the trip to town, taking three hours each way."

Pawnee Rock, c. 1880.

More Across Colorado

Greek Orzo Salad

1 pound orzo
4 ounces feta cheese, crumbled
¼ cup chopped fresh parsley
¼ cup chopped, roasted red peppers
1 red onion, thinly sliced
10 cherry tomatoes, halved
ground black pepper
½ cup fat-free chicken broth, *or* vegetable broth
2 tablespoons white wine vinegar
2 tablespoons lemon juice
2 tablespoons olive oil
1 clove garlic, minced
1 teaspoon dried oregano
4 cup baby spinach leaves
½ cup Greek olives, pitted and halved

Cooking time: 10 to 20 minutes
Serves: 8

Cook the orzo in a large pot of boiling water according to package directions.
Drain and rinse with cold water.
Drain again and place in a large bowl.
Add feta, parsley, red peppers, onion and tomatoes.
Season with the black pepper, to taste.
Toss to mix.
In a small bowl, combine the broth, vinegar, lemon juice, oil, garlic and oregano.
Add to the orzo mixture and toss to mix.
Serve on a bed of spinach leaves.
Top with olives.

More Across Colorado

3

"Fighting the Wolf Men" from the **Cheyenne Dog Soldier Ledgerbook,** *found in the aftermath of the battle of Summit Springs. This book of colored drawings by Cheyenne warrior-artists depicted the conflict on the Plains in 1865. The image shows Chief Tall Bull and Wolf with plenty of hair. Both men were killed at Summit Springs.*

More Across Colorado

INDIANS, PLAINS, AND BUFFALO

Thirty million buffalo once thundered over the prairies of the American West, with perhaps eight million on the southern plains. When native peoples acquired the horse from the Spaniards in the seventeenth century, the great buffalo herds suddenly became fair game. Hunting buffalo on their swift ponies, Plains Indians enjoyed immense prosperity, for the buffalo provided more than just a dependable food source. Clothing, tools, shelter, religious objects - all came from this great animal. Sustaining the buffalo was a sea of grass, predominantly grama, buffalo, and sage in eastern Colorado. This unique interaction between the land, animals, and people ended in the mid-nineteenth century with the coming of European cultures and technologies.

Marinated Asparagus

1 pound fresh asparagus, rinsed and trimmed

Marinade:
½ cup olive oil
¼ cup white wine vinegar
¼ cup fresh lemon juice
¼ cup chopped green onion – white and tender
    green part
2 tablespoons chopped parsley
½ teaspoon sugar
1 teaspoon dry mustard
½ teaspoon salt
¼ teaspoon black pepper
zest from 1 lemon
2 hard-boiled eggs, cut into wedges, optional
lettuce cups, optional
additional lemon zest for garnish

Cooking time: 10 minutes
Serves: 4

Blanch asparagus in boiling water until fork-tender.
Immediately plunge into ice-water bath to stop cooking process.
Pour off ice water, pat dry and place asparagus in a dish.
Prepare marinade in a blender *or* food processor. Blend until the mixture is emulsified.
Cover asparagus with marinade and refrigerate for a minimum of 3 hours.
Serve in lettuce cups if desired, with hard-boiled egg wedges and lemon zest as a garnish.

More Across Colorado

Attentive bidders at the Livestock Exchange, 1960s. Photograph courtesy The Livestock Exchange, Inc., Brush, Colorado.

AUCTIONEERING

Colorado stockmen have been auctioning off their herds in Brush since 1937, and the tradition remains alive and well. Auctioneers still chant out their commentary with jaw-numbing speed, and buyers still signal their bids with the subtlest of winks and nods. For all its color, though, auctioneering is a serious business: Ranchers' incomes ride on the outcome. The auctioneer must therefore be a master marketer, seasoning his rapid-fire rhetoric with persuasion and expert knowledge to secure the highest possible price. Brush's oldest cattle trade house, Brush Livestock of Colorado, boasts a 450-seat auditorium and pens for 6,000 cattle; the newest, Superior Livestock Auction, helped pioneer satellite auctioneering, in which bids may come in from around the world.

More Across Colorado

Marinated Broccoli and Cauliflower Salad

3 stalks of broccoli
1 small head cauliflower

Dressing:
1 cup olive oil
½ cup white wine vinegar
½ tablespoon dried oregano
½ tablespoon dried thyme
1 clove garlic, minced
1 teaspoon MSG, optional
salt and pepper to taste

Serves: 6 to 8

Cut broccoli and cauliflower into flowerets and place in bowl.
Whisk together all dressing ingredients.
Toss vegetables with dressing.
Cover and marinate 4 hours before serving.

More Across Colorado

Windmill and farm family.

BLOWIN' IN THE WIND

The windmill stands with the buffalo as the great symbol of the nineteenth-century American West. On the High Plains, water is scarce but wind constant. The genius of the western windmill, introduced to the Plains during the 1870s, is that it not only harnesses the wind to get at the hidden underground water, but it is small, multi-bladed, light, movable, self-regulating, easy to maintain, and inexpensive. Its uses are many: From pumping water for people, animals, and crops to powering tools like feed grinders, wood saws, churns, and corn shellers. No one knows how many windmills operate today - one estimate for the years between 1880 and 1930 is six million - but you can be sure that wherever you chance to be, one will be close by.

Mixed Baby Greens with Gorgonzola, Toasted Pecans and Apple

1 package mixed baby lettuce
½ cup crumbled Gorgonzola
1 apple, peeled and cut into small pieces
½ cup toasted chopped pecans

Dressing – yields 1 cup:
⅔ cup olive oil
3 tablespoons white wine vinegar
1 teaspoon dried whole oregano
¼ teaspoon salt
¼ teaspoon freshly ground pepper

Serves: 4

Combine the salad ingredients; set aside.
Combine all dressing ingredients in a jar; cover tightly and shake vigorously.
Mix and toss.

More Across Colorado

Prowers County dust storm, March 21, 1937. "In cities, semi-darkness at noonday, and street lights turned on. Auto headlights winking and blinking along the highways and the streets. For hours at a time, the sun was obscured by the dust-laden mist that hangs over the land." Springfield's *Democrat-Herald*, March 28, 1935.

More Across Colorado

THE DUST BOWL

Nowhere was the Great Depression greater than in southeastern Colorado. First the banks failed, ruining debt-ridden farmers. Then the rains stopped and the earth billowed, casting a pall over the prairies. Swirling dust jammed machinery, choked livestock, stripped cars and houses of paint. As the land dried up and blew away, so did people's lives: Baca County lost nearly half of its population between 1931 and 1936, and deposits at the Springfield bank fell a staggering 77 percent. Those who remained were certain that recovery was only a thundershower away: "Baca County can come back quicker than any other county in the United States," said one newspaper. But the healing did not begin until 1940, when local farmers finally harvested a wheat crop, the first since 1932.

Lost in a violent 1935 dust storm, a five-year-old Springfield boy wrapped his face in a handkerchief and curled up on the ground. Figuratively speaking, all of southeastern Colorado shared the experience, taking whatever shelter was available as the Depression ran its course. New Deal programs and community aid drives provided some relief, but the hardest-hit families had to resort to desperate measures. One mother retailored all her clothes to fit her children, then made herself a new wardrobe out of sackcloth. Another family survived a long, lean winter on nothing but corn meal and rabbit meat. Like the lost five-year-old, most Coloradans would survive the Dust Bowl, but only after enduring long days of acute fear and want.

Mostaccioli Salad

This recipe requires overnight refrigeration *

1-pound box of mostaccioli
olive oil

Dressing:
1½ cups cider vinegar
2 teaspoons prepared mustard
¾ to 1½ cups sugar
1 teaspoon garlic powder
1 teaspoon *each* salt and pepper, to taste

1 medium onion, chopped
1 medium cucumber, chopped but not peeled,
    or 3 stalks of celery, chopped
1 small jar of chopped pimento, *or* roasted
    peppers
¼ cup fresh, *or* dried parsley
1 small can sliced black olives, drained,
    optional
1 small bell pepper, chopped, optional

Cooking time: 10 minutes
Serves: 8

Cook pasta according to directions - **do not overcook.**
Coat pasta with olive oil until it looks shiny.

Dressing:
Mix a small amount of vinegar with the mustard to avoid lumps.
Dissolve the sugar in the vinegar-mustard mixture.
Whisk all dressing ingredients together.
Toss pasta with dressing.
* *Let stand overnight in the refrigerator, stirring occasionally.*

Assembly:
Toss pasta with selected vegetables and herbs.

Story: This is a favorite of my husband, Bob, a faithful Monday Morning volunteer in Books and Manuscripts. The recipe was given to me by a long-ago friend in Decatur, Illinois. *Mary Hartley*

More Across Colorado

A real estate office in Hugo proudly displays non-irrigated produce during the 1907 Lincoln County Dry Farming Jubilee and Festival. Courtesy Lincoln County Historical Society.

HOMESTEADING

Congress passed the Homestead Act in 1862, but a generation went by before settlers sought to claim these thirsty plains. The act's 160-acre allotment, though sufficient in the humid East, simply could not support a family on the arid Plains. But the 1872 Timber Culture Act and 1877 Desert Lands Act made larger parcels available, and as farmers mastered the art of dryland cultivation, eastern Colorado emerged as prime real estate. Pioneers began to trickle in during the 1890s and arrived in force after 1900; in 1907 the land office at Hugo led the nation in new claims. It had taken almost fifty years, but the government had finally devised a land policy suitable for the high prairies.

More Across Colorado

Orzo Tomato Arugula Salad

1 cup orzo
3 tablespoons olive oil
1 to 2 tablespoons balsamic vinegar
1 to 2 tablespoons lemon juice, optional
3 large tomatoes, peeled, seeded and diced
3 cups finely chopped arugula, *or* spinach
2 tablespoons chopped basil
⅓ cup finely chopped green onions, optional
salt to taste
6 tablespoons toasted pine nuts

Cooking time: 15 minutes
Serves: 4 to 6

Cook orzo according to package directions.
Rinse with cold water and chill.
Mix chilled orzo, olive oil, balsamic vinegar, and lemon juice if using, until orzo is evenly coated.
Add remaining ingredients, except pine nuts, and toss until blended.
Add pine nuts just before serving.
Serve as a delicious Mediterranean side dish.

Note: To toast pine nuts, place in a single layer on baking sheet and bake at 325° for 8 to 10 minutes or until lightly golden.

More Across Colorado

Prairie Schooners

SEA OF GRASS

Early white immigrants likened these rolling plains to great ocean waves. They described the treeless prairie, where sky and land seemed to merge, as a sea of grass. Wagons, with their white-topped covers, were likened to great-masted ships and called prairie schooners. Pioneers on the trail remarked on a sense of isolation, the constant wind, the sameness of the landscape, and how similar all this was to a long sea voyage. And like the oceans, the surrounding vista excited awe. It seemed vast and endless, although the Plains country stretched less than 600 miles between Denver and Kansas City. Still, as they traveled by oxen-drawn wagons, the trip could take fully six weeks, time enough to feel isolated, wind-swept, and lost in a sea of grass.

More Across Colorado

Romaine and Piñon Salad

Dressing:
2 garlic cloves
¼ teaspoon salt
1 teaspoon Dijon mustard
2 tablespoons red wine vinegar
⅓ cup olive oil
freshly ground pepper

Salad:
1 large head romaine, torn in pieces
grape tomatoes, optional
¼ cup grated Parmesan cheese
¼ cup piñon nuts, toasted

Cooking time: 10 to 15 minutes
Serves: 6

Dressing:
Boil garlic cloves in water just to cover for 10 minutes and drain.
In small non-aluminum bowl, mash the garlic and salt together with the back of a fork.
Whisk in the mustard and vinegar.
Slowly whisk in the oil until the dressing is thick.
Add the pepper.

Assembly:
Place lettuce and tomatoes, if using, in a large salad bowl and toss with the dressing.
Sprinkle the cheese and nuts over the greens and toss again.
Serve immediately.

More Across Colorado

"The plazas are constructed of mud, and in the way of comfort, they are really desirable, being cool, like cellars, in warm weather, and in winter close and warm." Matthew C. Field, nineteenth-century newspaperman.

More Across Colorado

HISPANO PLAZAS

As you travel the Highway of Legends between Trinidad and La Veta, look for remnants of Hispano *plazas* - villages - along the river. In 1862, twelve Hispano families came over from northern New Mexico. "There was plenty of room and opportunities for [a man] to pick land just as it suited him anywhere," said Don Felipe Baca, the group's leader. The settlers built *plazas* with thick outside adobe walls as a defense against raiding Indians. Other Hispano settlers also came until there was "scarcely a mile along the stream in which you do not find a ranch or two." Daily life in the settlement was filled with hard work, but the people found time for religious celebrations, fiestas, and horse racing. After the 1870s, coal mines and railroads brought changes to the area and largely overshadowed the Hispano settlements. By the 1930s most of these settlements had receded into memory.

Romaine Chiffonade with Pesto Vinaigrette

1 purple onion, cut into slices and separated
    into rings
3 cups shredded romaine lettuce
2 tablespoons pine nuts
2 tablespoons chopped fresh basil
1 tablespoon minced garlic
¼ cup balsamic vinegar
½ teaspoon cracked pepper
½ cup olive oil

Combine onions and lettuce in a large bowl.
Process pine nuts and next 4 ingredients in a blender until smooth, stopping once to scrape down sides.
Turn blender on high; add oil in a slow steady stream.
Pour dressing over lettuce and onion; toss gently.
Serve immediately.

Serves: 8

Southwestern Salad

1 can ranch-style pinto beans with jalapeño
    chiles, rinsed and drained
1 can shoe-peg corn, drained
1 small can sliced black olives, drained
1 red bell pepper, chopped
1 large head romaine lettuce in bite-size pieces
8-ounce package Mexican-style shredded
    cheese
1 small bottle Catalina salad dressing
1 small package chili/cheese flavored corn
    chips

Combine first 6 ingredients.
Toss with dressing.
Just before serving, mix in chips.

Serves: 6

More Across Colorado

Dolores Baca

Frank Bloom

More Across Colorado

BACA AND BLOOM

Two families, two cultures, one city. Felipe and Dolores Baca, wealthy Hispanos who led a group of pioneers to Trinidad, brought a sense of community to this settlement on the Santa Fe Trail. They donated land for the townsite and supported the Catholic school and church. As farmers, ranchers, and property owners, the Bacas also influenced Trinidad's economic growth. Frank Bloom, an equally important figure, embodied the Yankee spirit of individual enterprise. As merchant, banker, cattle baron, and owner of a coal mine, he amassed a personal fortune and influenced the industries that sustained Trinidad for generations. The Baca House and Bloom Mansion, both historic landmarks and museums, stand together as fitting tributes to two prominent families from Trinidad's earliest years.

Spinach Salad Supreme

6-ounce package baby spinach
½ cup crumbled Feta cheese
1 medium-size ripe avocado
1 cup fresh blueberries
1 red onion cut in rings
½ cup toasted almond slices
poppy seed dressing to taste

Cooking time: 8 to 10 minutes
Serves: 6

Mix first 4 ingredients shortly before serving time.
Arrange sliced onion rings and toasted almonds on top.
Serve poppy seed dressing on the side.

Note: To toast almonds, bake at 300° for 8 to 10 minutes, stirring often as they burn easily.

Tomatoes Lutece

8 large, firm, ripe tomatoes
¼ cup chopped parsley
½ teaspoon chopped garlic
1 teaspoon salt
1 teaspoon sugar
¼ teaspoon pepper
¼ cup olive oil
2 tablespoons vinegar
2 teaspoons prepared mustard

Serves: 8 to 10

Slice tomatoes into thick, even slices and set aside.
Combine remaining ingredients into a small jar and shake well.
Place one layer of tomatoes in a shallow dish and cover with half of dressing. Place the other half of the tomatoes on top, and cover with remaining dressing.
Let stand at room temperature at least 20 minutes before serving.

More Across Colorado

It took hours to heat a **horno** *to the temperature required for baking and cooking.*

THE MADRID PLACITA

In the spring of 1862, Hilario Madrid stood on a grassy bench. The bench overlooked the river valley and the hills beyond. This was where he would build his home. He set about constructing a *placita*, a single-family compound. Built of adobe - sand mixed with straw and water and dried in the sun - the *placita* included an L-shaped main building with walls twenty-one inches thick and a sod roof. Inside were the family units, *sala* (living room) and storage room. Across a patio stood the cattle sheds and a shelter for domestic animals. Nearby was the *horno*, a beehive-shaped oven used to bake bread, cook meat, and dry corn. For almost a century, this secure *placita* was home to the Madrid family, including José Miguel Madrid, who was elected to the Colorado State Senate in 1932.

More Across Colorado

Spinach Tortellini Salad

Dressing:
¼ cup olive oil
¼ cup wine vinegar
2 tablespoons grated Parmesan cheese
1 tablespoon chopped fresh basil, *or* 1 teaspoon
        dried
Salad:
1½-ounce package dried cheese-filled tortellini
4 cups fresh spinach, torn into bite-size pieces
¼ cup bacon bits
1 medium-size bell pepper, cut into strips
additional grated Parmesan cheese

Serves: 4

Shake oil, vinegar, cheese and basil in tightly covered container.

Salad:
Cook tortellini as directed on package.
Rinse in cold water and drain.
Pour dressing over tortellini.
Cover and chill for about 2 hours.
Toss tortellini and remaining ingredients.
Serve with freshly ground pepper and additional Parmesan cheese if desired.

More Across Colorado

"UNCLE DICK" WOOTTON

Richens Lacy "Uncle Dick" Wootton, 1816-1893.

More Across Colorado

Today's highway over Raton Pass parallels the toll road built by "Uncle Dick" Wootton in 1866. Wootton improved some twenty-seven miles of the toughest part of the road. "There were hillsides to cut down, he said, "rocks to blast and remove, and bridges to build by the score. I built the road, however, and made it a good one." He erected a tollgate in front of his house and initially charged $1.50 for one wagon or buggy and 25 cents for a "horseman," prices that he changed for time to time. But Wootton always allowed the Indians to use the toll road free of charge. In 1879 the Atchison, Topeka & Santa Fe Railroad bought the right of way from Wootton. The following year, the railroad built all the way to Santa Fe, and the era of the Santa Fe Trail came to an end.

Richens Lacy Wootton, known as Uncle Dick, was born on May 6, 1816, in Mecklenburg County, Virginia. Those who knew him said he was a natural-born frontiersman who needed room and breathing space. "He did not like towns," said an acquaintance. "He did not like being jostled on wooden sidewalks." At age nineteen he traveled west and hired on with William Bent to move caravans of wagons down the Santa Fe Trail. For the next fifty-seven years, Wootton earned his living as a trader, trapper, hunter, farmer, freighter, merchant, and road builder. In the home that Wootton built near his toll road, stagecoach passengers always found a hot lunch waiting, along with an abundance of good stories.

Tortellini Salad

12-ounce package dried cheese-filled tortellini
¼ cup olive oil
¼ cup wine vinegar
2 tablespoons grated Parmesan cheese
1 tablespoon chopped fresh basil, *or* 1 teaspoon
    dried
4 cups fresh spinach, torn into bite-size pieces
¼ cup bacon bits
1 medium bell pepper, cut into strips
freshly ground pepper to taste, optional
additional grated Parmesan cheese, optional

Cooking time: tortellini package directions
Serves: 4

Cook tortellini as directed on package.
Rinse in cold water and drain.
Shake oil, vinegar, cheese and basil in tightly covered container.
Pour this dressing over tortellini.
Cover and chill for about 2 hours.
Add remaining ingredients to tortellini and toss.
Serve with pepper and additional Parmesan if desired.

More Across Colorado

Lamar, c. 1900.

LAMAR

The speculators who founded Lamar required a federal land office and a railroad depot to ensure their venture's success. They secured the land office by naming their town after the sitting secretary of the Interior: L.Q.C. Lamar. The depot they stole from cattleman A.R. Black. When Black refused to sell his station, which sat three miles away, the Lamar group had him summoned to Pueblo and then hauled the structure to the new townsite in his absence. Lots went on sale May 24, 1886, and saloons and real estate agencies were open by week's end. The *Lamar Register* appeared in June, and stores, schools, and a church soon followed. The population approached 1,000 by December 1886, when Lamar elected its first government. All this took only seven months.

Tropical Chicken Salad

*This recipe needs refrigeration for at least 4
hours and probably overnight.* *

2 whole bone-in chicken breasts with skin
1 tart green apple, peeled and cut into 1-inch
    pieces
1 cup diced fresh pineapple
1 cup seedless green grapes, halved
3 tablespoons chopped bottled chutney
1 cup mayonnaise
1½ teaspoons curry powder
salt to taste
3 ripe cantaloupes, prepared just before
    assembling the salad
Bibb lettuce leaves, washed, dried and chilled
1 cup coarsely chopped macadamia nuts

Cooking time: 20 minutes
Serves: 6

Poach chicken breasts, cool, skin, remove bone and chop into 1½-inch pieces.
In a bowl, combine chicken, apple, pineapple and grapes.
Combine the chutney, mayonnaise, curry powder and salt.
Pour dressing over chicken mixture and blend well.
* *Cover and refrigerate at least 4 hours, preferably overnight.*

When ready to assemble, cut each cantaloupe in half, seed and re-move peel.
Slice a small amount off the bottom of each half so it won't roll.
Place Bibb lettuce leaves on 6 salad plates.
Place a prepared cantaloupe half on top of lettuce leaf.
Place equal amounts of chicken-salad mixture in hollow of each cantaloupe.
Sprinkle macadamia nuts over the top of the salad.

More Across Colorado

Big Timbers on the Arkansas River, *from a sketch by Lt. James William Abert, 1845.*

BIG TIMBERS

At the height of the Santa Fe Trail, this spot was one of the liveliest way stations. The Big Timbers, a thick belt of giant cottonwoods, stretched along the Arkansas River from here almost to Las Animas. Indians, trappers, and freighters relished this Plains paradise, and William Bent built his second trading post here in 1853, two decades before the railroad began to replace traffic on the trail. The tracks wiped out the old road as they advanced, bringing soldiers, settlers, and cattlemen. These pioneers decimated the game herds, displaced the Indians, and harvested Big Timbers for building material. By the turn of the century, the woody expanse and active trade route were largely gone.

More Across Colorado

24-Hour Cabbage Salad

*This salad must be refrigerated for 24 hours before serving. ***

Dressing:
1 cup vinegar
¾ cup salad oil
1¼ cups sugar

Salad:
1 large head cabbage, shredded
1 green onion, chopped
1 small onion, chopped, *or* 1 bunch green
　　　　onions, sliced
1 teaspoon salt
½ teaspoon celery salt (or more to taste)
freshly ground black pepper, to taste, optional

Cooking time:　10 minutes
Serves:　6 to 8

Bring dressing ingredients to a boil.
Mix salad ingredients.
Cool to room temperature.
Pour enough dressing over the salad ingredients to moisten as desired.
Store any remaining dressing in the refrigerator.
Stir well.
* Refrigerate for 24 hours before serving.

Stir well before serving.

More Across Colorado

INDIAN WARS 1864 - 1869

Sand Creek Massacre *by Robert Lindneux, 1936. The massacre united the Plains tribes in an unprecedented war against white soldiers and civilians along the South Platte River. The war ended with the Battle of Summit Springs.*

On November 29, 1864, in southeastern Colorado, U.S. Volunteer troops attacked Black Kettle's peaceful band of Cheyenne Indians at Sand Creek. In retaliation for the massacre and mutilation of 163 Cheyenne men, women, and children, Cheyenne warriors with their Arapaho and Sioux allies struck military and civilian targets along the South Platte River Trail. On January 7, 1865, some 1,500 warriors attacked stage and telegraph stations, ranches, and wagon trains on a 100-mile front between Julesburg, Colorado - ninety miles northeast of Akron - and Denver. These great South Platte River raids closed Denver to the outside world and resulted in over 250 Army and civilian deaths, diverted 8,000 Union troops from battle lines in the East, and cost the government some $30 million.

More Across Colorado

Turkey Cream Soup

¼ cup butter, *or* margarine
2 tablespoons chopped onion
½ to 1 teaspoon curry powder
3 cups turkey, *or* chicken, broth
1 cup diced potatoes
½ cup diced carrots
½ cup celery, sliced diagonally
salt
pepper
1 cup diced cooked turkey
½ teaspoon oregano, or to taste
1 tablespoon minced parsley
1⅔ cups light cream, *or* 14½ ounces evaporated
    milk
2 tablespoons flour
1 package frozen French-style green beans,
    optional
brandy, optional

Cooking time: 45 minutes to 1 hour
Serves: 4 to 6

Melt butter in good-sized saucepan *or* Dutch kettle.
Cook onion in butter until transparent.
Stir in curry powder and cook another minute or so.
Stir in broth, potatoes, carrots, celery and seasoning to taste.
Bring to a boil and then cook on very low heat for about 15 minutes.
Add turkey, oregano and parsley.
If using green beans, they should be added at the same time as the turkey.
Continue cooking another 15 minutes, or until vegetables are barely tender.
Combine cream, *or* milk, and flour, stirring into soup gently until well blended.
Soup should be slightly thickened. Heat thoroughly, **but do not allow to boil.**
One teaspoon of brandy may be put in bowl when serving.

More Across Colorado

OVER THE PASS

Crossing Raton Pass was the hardest part of the journey along the Mountain Route of the Santa Fe Trail. An early traveler said the road climbed through a narrow defile filled with boulders and "sudden turns that gave you a glimpse of the green valley below." To pass the overhanging rocks, wagons crawled along the edge of steep drop-offs. Thunderstorms were often violent, and summer rains washed out whole sections of road. While making the trip with her trader husband in 1846, Susan Magoffin wrote in her journal: "…almost every fifty or [one] hundred yards there are large stones, or steep little hillocks, just the thing to bounce a wagon [wheel] up, unless there is the most careful driving."

Susan Shelby Magoffin, 1827-1855. In 1846 Magoffin accompanied her husband and his trade caravan along the Santa Fe Trail. Her diary of that journey offers a rare glimpse into daily life on the trail.

More Across Colorado

Acorn Squash

2 acorn squash
4 tablespoons butter
4 tablespoons brown sugar

Cooking time: 1 hour in oven, 7 to 8
        minutes in microwave
Serves: 4

Split acorn squash in half and remove seeds.
Place cut-side down in a shallow pan with about 1 inch of water.
Bake at 350° until fork tender.
Remove from oven, turn squash over so hollow side is facing up.
Add 1 tablespoon butter and 1 tablespoon brown sugar to each half.
Return squash to oven until butter and sugar melt – 3 to 5 minutes.

May also bake squash in microwave as follows:
Pierce whole squash with fork in several places.
Do not cut apart.
Place on paper plate and cook for 7 to 8 minutes.
After squash is cooked, carefully cut in half and remove seeds.
Add 1 tablespoon butter and 1 tablespoon brown sugar to each half.
Return to microwave for 1 to 2 minutes until butter and sugar melt.

More Across Colorado

For Colorado miners, a pressing concern was the dangerous nature of their work. Despite efforts of rescue teams such as this one (c. 1910), over 1,700 miners died in Colorado mines between 1884 and 1912.

LIFE OF THE COAL MINER

Colorado coal miners literally risked their lives on the job. Hundreds died each year in explosions, cave-ins, and other accidents caused by company negligence. Lung disease ran rampant among them. Their pay - a typical wage in the 1910s was 35 cents per ton of ore mined (roughly $10 a week) - did not come close to offsetting these hazards. Worse, their employers controlled every aspect of their lives. Required to live in company housing, send their children to company schools, and buy equipment with scrip at the company store, they were for all intents and purposes mere property. No wonder 90 percent of southern Colorado's miners heeded the call to strike in September 1913 - and were willing to die for their cause.

More Across Colorado

Baked Artichoke Hearts

14-ounce can artichoke hearts
5 slices of bread
3 to 4 tablespoons grated Romano cheese
1 teaspoon parsley
1 clove garlic, chopped
¼ teaspoon salt
¼ teaspoon pepper
small can chopped jalapeño peppers, add to
     taste
1 egg, beaten
olive oil

Cooking time: 30 minutes
Serves: 6 to 8

Drain and rinse artichoke hearts; drain again and dry on paper towels.
Blend or chop the bread in a blender.
Place crumbs in a pie plate. Set aside.
Mix cheese, parsley, garlic, salt, pepper and enough jalapeño peppers to suit your taste.
Add the beaten egg to the cheese-parsley mixture.
Dip each artichoke heart into the batter, then roll in breadcrumb mixture.
Pat the crumb mixture firmly around each artichoke heart.
Place in a baking dish and drizzle olive oil over the top.
Bake at 350° until brown.

Frances Owens
Colorado's First Lady
Office of the First Lady
136 State Capitol
Denver, Colorado

More Across Colorado

The Ludlow tent colony prior to the fire of April 20, 1914.

THE LUDLOW MASSACRE

By April 1914, the striking coal miners encamped at Ludlow had nothing to lose but their lives. Poor, powerless, largely immigrant, they had held out for seven months against mighty Colorado Fuel & Iron, joining a statewide action led by the United Mine Workers. Stung by lost profits (and by union attacks against company property), CF&I demanded government intervention; accordingly, state troopers were dispatched to the tent colony, ostensibly as peacekeepers. On April 20, 1914, shots rang out at Ludlow and fire swept the camp. At the end of the day, seventeen civilians lay dead, including two women and eleven children who suffocated while hiding in a pit beneath a smoldering tent. These tragic killings outraged the public nationwide and marked the beginning of U.S. labor reform.

 *More Across Colorado*

Baked Cabbage

3 cups shredded cabbage
¾ cup cream
1 tablespoon sugar
½ cup chopped walnuts
½ cup bread crumbs
1 cup shredded sharp cheddar cheese

Cooking time: 45 to 50 minutes
Serves: 4 to 6

Place cabbage in a greased 2-quart baking dish
Combine cream, sugar and nuts; pour over cabbage.
Top with bread crumbs.
Bake at 325° for 45 to 50 minutes.
Sprinkle with cheese; bake just until cheese is melted.

Broccoli and Cauliflower Casserole

4 large stalks of broccoli
1 large head of cauliflower
10¾-ounce can cream of mushroom soup, *or*
    favorite condensed "cream of" soup
½ cup mayonnaise
2 cups grated sharp cheddar cheese
2-ounce jar diced pimentos, drained
1 tablespoon fresh lemon juice
1 to 1½ cups crushed cheese crackers, optional
¼ cup, slivered almonds, toasted, optional

Cooking time: 35 to 40 minutes
Serves: 8

Separate broccoli and cauliflower into small flowerets.
Steam until crisp tender. Place in ice-water bath to stop cooking.
Drain well.
Mix soup, mayonnaise, grated cheese, pimentos and lemon juice;
blend with well-drained vegetables.
Spoon into a greased 2-quart baking dish.
If using cheese cracker crumbs and/or almonds, sprinkle evenly
over the top.
Bake at 350° about 30 minutes or until heated through.
Serve immediately.

More Across Colorado

Settling near Pueblo in 1853, Mountain Man and trader Charles Autobees personified the integration of cultures in the Upper Arkansas Valley where family and friends crossed all racial, national, and ethnic lines. Autobees spoke English, Spanish, Cheyenne, Arapaho, Sioux, and Navajo fluently.

BORDERLAND

The 1819 Adams-Oñis Treaty fixed the boundary between the U.S. and Spain at the Arkansas River, formalizing a centuries-old convention: The Arkansas had always been a border. Neighboring Indian tribes fronted tensely on this crucial waterway, whose wealth of resources (water, timber, pasture, game) were essential for survival. The colonial powers, too, jostled for control of the river, which came to represent the proverbial line in the sand. Any breach drew the fiercest resistance. Spain was particularly vigilant, ignoring French and American travelers north of the Arkansas but treating all who ventured south of it (including Lt. Zebulon Pike) as hostile invaders. With America's 1848 conquest of northern Mexico and the removal of the Arapahos and Cheyennes in 1865, the river finally ceased to divide. For the first time in perhaps 1,000 years, the Arkansas served a single country. Today, it remains a cultural border of the American Southwest.

More Across Colorado

Broccoli Onion Deluxe

10-ounce package frozen cut broccoli
2 medium-size onions, cut in large chunks
4 tablespoons butter, divided
2 tablespoons flour
¼ teaspoon salt
dash pepper
1 cup milk
3-ounce package cream cheese
4 ounces (½ cup) sharp American cheese,
    shredded
½ cup bread crumbs

Cooking time: 35 minutes
Serves: 4 to 6

Cook frozen broccoli according to package instructions. Drain.
Cook onions in boiling salted water until tender. Drain.
In a saucepan, melt 2 tablespoons of the butter.
Blend in the flour with the salt and a dash of pepper.
Add milk slowly.
Cook, stirring, until thick and bubbly.
Reduce heat.
Add in cream cheese, stirring until smooth.
Place broccoli and onions in a 1½-quart baking dish.
Pour sauce over broccoli and lightly mix.
Top with shredded cheese.
Melt remaining butter and toss with the bread crumbs.
Sprinkle buttered crumbs around the edge of the casserole.
Bake uncovered at 350° for 30 minutes.

More Across Colorado

CAMP AMACHE

Barely a trace remains of Camp Amache, a federal "relocation center" that housed Japanese-Americans during World War II. The camp opened in August 1942 and almost instantly became Colorado's tenth-largest city, with a peak population of 7,500. In some ways Amache was like any other American community, with its own government, businesses, newspaper, school system, hospital, farms, and fire and police departments. But the residents were essentially prisoners: They were brought against their will and could not leave without permission. Over time, many were allowed to resettle nearby; some 2,000 stayed in Colorado after the war. Others volunteered for military service as soldiers, nurses, and interpreters. And thirty-one died fighting for the United States in World War II.

Camp Amache

More Across Colorado

Broccoli Rice Casserole

1 package frozen chopped broccoli
½ cup butter
1 chopped onion
2 cups shredded cheddar cheese
4-ounce can diced green chiles
1 cup Minute rice
1 can cream of mushroom soup

Cooking time: 30 minutes
Serves: 6 to 8

Grease a 1½-quart baking dish.
Cook broccoli as directed on package, *or* cook fresh broccoli until fork-tender.
Combine all ingredients and pour into prepared dish.
Cover dish and bake at 350° for 30 minutes.
May add ham or chicken to make this an easy one-dish meal.

Cardamom Peas

¼ cup water
1½ cups freshly shelled green peas, *or* frozen
        peas
½ teaspoon salt
¼ teaspoon pepper
¼ teaspoon cardamom
1 tablespoon parsley
a few chives

Cooking time: 20 minutes
Serves: 4 to 6

Bring water to boil.
Add peas.
Cover and cook until tender.
Drain all but 1 tablespoon of the water.
Toss peas with remaining ingredients and serve immediately.

More Across Colorado

La Veta and Spanish Peaks, 1884.

SPANISH PEAKS

Miguel Oñate may have built a fort beneath the Spanish Peaks as early as 1598 - but maybe not. Another Spaniard, New Mexico Governor Antonio de Valverde, supposedly erected a supply post nearby in 1719. Who can say for sure? So many legends surround these mythic mountains that it's impossible to tell fact from fiction. The Utes called them Huajatolla ("the breasts of the earth," wellsprings of life) and believed ghosts and vengeful gods populated the slopes. Spanish explorers thought the Peaks harbored forbidden treasures, but they, too, feared the mountains' power - and wrath. One witness swore that fire and steam shot forth from the crest. Although travelers were guided by these distinctive landmarks for many centuries, most kept a respectful distance away - just in case the legends might be true.

More Across Colorado

Carrots Elegante

1 pound carrots, thinly sliced
¼ cup golden raisins
3 tablespoons honey
1 tablespoon lemon juice
¼ teaspoon ground ginger
¼ cup sliced almonds

Cooking time: 35 minutes
Serves: 4

Preheat oven to 375°.
Cook carrots covered in a half-inch of boiling water for 8 minutes.
Drain.
Place carrots in 1-quart baking dish.
Stir in everything but the almonds.
Bake 35 minutes uncovered, stirring occasionally.
Top with almonds.

More Across Colorado

THE TRAIL—A THING OF THE PAST.

A trail herd of Texas Longhorns.

TRAIL DAYS

It was that simple: Drive the $5 steer to the $50 market and pocket the difference. Easy money. In post-Civil War Texas, where cattle outnumbered people six to one, almost anyone could cobble together a presentable herd and prod it north. From the late 1860s through the end of the century, hundreds of thousands of Texas steers hit the trail annually. Roughly a quarter of them came through on the Goodnight-Loving Trail. Though rougher, drier, and more exposed than routes into Kansas, the Goodnight-Loving Trail provided access to unclaimed grasslands and growing consumer markets as well as railheads. Thanks largely to this hoof-beaten highway, Colorado's cattle population grew from a scattered handful in 1860 to more than a million by 1880.

More Across Colorado

Cauliflower Mornay

1 large head cauliflower

Mornay Sauce:
3 tablespoons butter
3 tablespoons flour
2 cups milk
¾ teaspoon salt
¼ teaspoon pepper
2 tablespoons cold butter cut into small pieces
1 cup freshly grated Parmesan

Topping:
1 cup freshly grated bread crumbs
¼ cup melted butter

Cooking time: 30 to 45 minutes
Serves: 6 to 8

Steam cauliflower until tender and arrange in a 2-quart baking dish.

Mornay Sauce:
Melt the 3 tablespoons of butter in top of double-boiler over boiling water.
Stir in flour with a wooden spoon until smooth.
Gradually add milk, stirring constantly.
Cook until sauce is thick.
Stir in salt and pepper.
Stir in the 2 tablespoons cut-up butter and the Parmesan.
Beat with wooden spoon until butter is melted.
Spoon Mornay over cauliflower.

Topping:
Combine bread crumbs and butter.
Sprinkle buttered crumbs over cauliflower.
Place under hot broiler until crumbs are lightly browned.

More Across Colorado

Colonel Charles Goodnight

CHARLES GOODNIGHT

In pioneering the first cattle trail from Texas to Colorado, Charles Goodnight risked everything. He and partner Oliver Loving drove 2,000 Longhorns over nearly 1,000 miles of trackless prairie in 1866, enduring Indian raids, dust storms, and four waterless days in the Texas Panhandle. Their reward: A $12,000 sale and the eternal gratitude of the nation's stockmen. Goodnight settled at Rock Canon Ranch, bringing 30,000 head into Colorado. An economic downturn in the late 1870s ruined him financially, and he returned to Texas to build a new cattle empire. But this inspirational figure left a rich legacy in Colorado's economy and lore.

Charles Goodnight

More Across Colorado

Colcannon

8 potatoes
¾ cup hot scalded milk
6 green onions, chopped
1½ cups finely chopped, boiled green cabbage
2 tablespoons butter, melted
1 tablespoon chopped parsley
salt
pepper

Cooking time: 20 minutes
Serves: 6 to 8

Boil potatoes and mash.
Add hot scalded milk and green onions and beat until fluffy.
Toss the cabbage with the butter.
Add the cabbage and parsley to the potatoes, blending well.
Season generously with salt and pepper to taste.

Note: For an Irish menu to go with Colcannon, try tea, corned beef, and baby carrots cooked whole and unpeeled. You'll have the colors of the Irish flag: White in the potatoes, green in the cabbage, orange in the carrots. Plus Irish Soda Bread and Trifle for dessert.

Story: If you're of Celtic heritage and wear green on St. Paddy's day, you'll have a dinner of corned beef and cabbage on or near March 17. Since I am and I do, I have in more recent years varied this celebratory menu with another Irish dish: Colcannon. And, of course, I serve it with corned beef. Although Colcannon is traditionally served at Halloween, it works for me on St. Patrick's Day as well. One summer I was attending a James Joyce seminar at Trinity College in Dublin, and I came across *My Irish Cook Book*, a compilation of traditional Irish recipes by Monica Sheridan, a Julia Childs of the Emerald Isle. This is from her book.
J. P. (Judy) Atwater

More Across Colorado

COLORADO FUEL & IRON

Among Colorado's corporate citizens, few have been as important as Colorado Fuel & Iron (CF&I). Created by merger in 1879, this industrial colossus soon ranked as the largest steel producer west of the Mississippi and one of the 10 largest in the world. CF&I's billowing smokestacks often darkened the skies over Pueblo, but those plumes of exhaust brought sunshine to the region's economy. By 1904 the company, now bankrolled by the Rockefeller and Gould families, was Colorado's largest employer (with 17,000 workers) and heaviest taxpayer. As a fully integrated steel and fuel producer, CF&I controlled quarries, mines, smelters, railroads, workshops, land companies, and banks throughout the West. Along with these interests, CF&I's prodigious output of steel - everything from wire and rails to rivets and nails - and vast financial reserves constituted a framework for Colorado's growth, the girders and beams of development.

Colorado Fuel & Iron, Minnequa Steel Plant.

More Across Colorado

Corn Green Bean Casserole

14-ounce can white corn, drained
15-ounce can French-style green beans, drained
½ cup chopped celery
½ cup chopped onion
2-ounce jar pimentos, drained, optional
½ cup sour cream
1 cup shredded cheddar cheese
1 can cream of celery soup

Topping:
4 tablespoons butter
½ to 1 cup Ritz cracker crumbs
¼ to ½ cup slivered, *or* chopped, almonds

Cooking time: 35 to 40 minutes
Serves: 6

Mix first 8 ingredients.
Place in a greased casserole dish.
In a saucepan, melt butter and add cracker crumbs.
Sprinkle cracker crumbs on top of casserole just to cover, not too thickly.
Sprinkle almonds on top.
Bake uncovered at 350° until browned – 35 to 40 minutes.
If using a glass dish, bake at 325°.

More Across Colorado

In 1892, fifty-one trains a day came through Union Depot, 164,718 pieces of baggage were handled, and 103,114 tickets totaling $568,639 were sold.

UNION AVENUE AND DEPOT

Erected in 1889, Pueblo's Union Depot was an emblem of civic pride, complete with Romanesque architecture, stained-glass windows, and a 150-foot-high clock tower. For sheer grandeur, few Colorado buildings could match it. And few streets could match the bustle of Union Avenue, a teeming promenade lined with hotels, shops, and restaurants. It was the flourishing heart of a flourishing city. However, the 1921 flood (which soaked the depot in eleven feet of water), the Great Depression, and the railroad's postwar decline took their toll; by 1971 Union Depot stood empty, and the once-handsome Avenue was vacant and deteriorating. But Puebloans fought to restore luster to the neighborhood. Designated a National Historic District in 1982, Union Avenue is again a prestige destination, and the rehabilitated depot sparkles, wearing its heritage proudly.

More Across Colorado

Corn Bread Casserole

14¾-ounce can cream-style corn
15-ounce can yellow corn, drained
8½-ounce box cornbread mix
¼ cup butter, melted
1 cup sour cream
2 eggs
5 green onions, chopped
2 4-ounce cans diced green chiles

Cooking time: 45 minutes to 1 hour
Serves: 6

Grease a 3-quart baking dish.
In large bowl, combine the 2 corns, cornbread mix, butter, sour cream, eggs, onions and green chiles.
Spoon into a prepared dish.
Bake at 375° for 45 minutes to 1 hour, until knife inserted in middle comes out clean.

Creamy Mashed Potatoes

2½ pounds potatoes, peeled and quartered
3-ounce package cream cheese
1 teaspoon fresh chives, chopped
¼ teaspoon garlic salt
⅛ teaspoon salt
⅛ teaspoon pepper
2 tablespoons butter
1 cup heavy cream

Cooking time: 45 minutes
Serves: 6

Cook potatoes until tender. Using mixer, mash at medium speed.
Add cream cheese, chives, salt, pepper and 1 tablespoon of the butter. Using mixer, beat at medium speed until blended.
Beat in heavy cream.
Spoon into an 8-inch-square baking dish.
Dot with remaining butter.
Bake at 350° for 45 minutes.
If refrigerated prior to baking, bring to room temperature before placing in oven.

More Across Colorado

Cripple Creek c. 1890.

More Across Colorado

PIKES PEAK

During his famous 1806-07 expedition, Lt. Zebulon M. Pike estimated the elevation of Grand Peak at 19,000 feet. The mountain, which now bears the intrepid lieutenant's name, actually stands 14,110 feet high, but its stature in the American psyche is immeasurably higher. As the first mountain to appear to pioneers traveling west, Pikes Peak was a beacon of hope, a harbinger of frontier freedom and boundless opportunity. "Pikes Peak or Bust" became a Gold Rush mantra, a prayer for deliverance into the Promised Land. Katharine Lee Bates inscribed those sentiments in *America the Beautiful*, which she conceived atop the summit in 1893. Like Everest, Fuji, and Kilimanjaro, Pikes Peak is more than a mountain - it's a symbol of national majesty.

Pikes Peak anchors a region of riches. Native peoples treasured this land for its bountiful game and therapeutic hot springs, and nineteenth-century Mountain Men trapped a fortune in fur here. But that most coveted of rewards - gold - proved an elusive find. Spanish explorers investigated claims that rivers of gold flowed off Pikes Peak, and American prospectors made some modest digs at Colorado City (briefly considered a territorial capital). They didn't strike paydirt until 1890, but the wait was well worth it. The Cripple Creek gold rush was one of the greatest in U.S. history. By the time it ended, Colorado Springs had more millionaires per capita than anywhere else in America. Now cherished for its scenic splendor, Pikes Peak country remains a land of priceless assets.

Crunchy Celery

4 heaping cups sliced celery
1 can cream of chicken soup, undiluted
1 can sliced water chestnuts, drained
2-ounce package slivered almonds, toasted
soy sauce

Cooking time: 30 minutes
Serves 6.

Place celery in pan of salted water and bring to boil. Let cook 2 minutes. Drain well; place in mixing bowl. Stir in soup, pimento and water chestnuts. Pour into a greased baking dish.
Sprinkle almonds on top. Bake at 350°, uncovered, for 30 minutes. Serve warm, with soy sauce to pass.
If prepared in advance, do not put almonds on top until dish is ready to be put in oven.

Fried Cabbage

¼ cup oil
1 large onion, chopped coarsely
1 large head of cabbage, sliced ¼-inch-thick
salt and pepper to taste
¼ cup sugar, to taste

This recipe is to taste, and the ingredients are approximate.

Cooking time: 25 minutes
Serves: 4 to 6

Pour the oil in a hot skillet. Add onions and only sweat them – **do not brown**. Add cabbage and stir onions into it. Simmer with the lid on. You may have to add a little cabbage at a time depending on the size of your skillet. Salt and pepper to taste.
Do not add liquid, as the cabbage makes its own as it breaks down. Stir often. As the cabbage starts to brown, add the sugar and stir well. Fry another 5 minutes. Do not let the cabbage brown too much. Remove from heat. Serve immediately.

Note: This is excellent with pork chops, mashed potatoes and gravy, and corn bread. You may like to try the cabbage with a little of the gravy – and want to serve with homemade apple sauce.

More Across Colorado

Bent's Old Fort National Historic Site on the Arkansas River. Photograph courtesy of John Russell.

BENT'S OLD FORT

On the Arkansas River, near La Junta, stands a reconstruction of Bent's Old Fort, the unique creation of three cultures: Anglo-American, Cheyenne, and Mexican. Ceran St. Vrain and the brothers William and Charles Bent conceived the idea of a trading empire centered here on the Arkansas River. The Cheyennes picked the fort's site and agreed to supply Bent, St. Vrain & Co. with buffalo robes, a mainstay of the fur trade. Hispanos from New Mexico built the fort using adobe construction techniques especially suited for this region. Bent's Old Fort flourished from 1834 until 1849, when it was abandoned.

More Across Colorado

Great Green Beans

*This recipe can be prepared a day ahead. *

1 teaspoon olive oil
1 onion, finely chopped
1 clove garlic, finely chopped
2 ounces thin-sliced prosciutto, *or* bacon, finely
        chopped
1½ pounds green beans
salt to taste

Cooking time: 15 minutes
Serves: 6 to 8

In a frying pan over high heat, stir oil, onion, garlic and prosciutto until onion is lightly browned – 5 to 7 minutes.
Keep warm.
Meanwhile, in a large pan (4 to 5 quarts), bring 3 quarts of water to a boil over high heat.
Add beans and cook, uncovered, until tender-crisp when pierced – 6 to 12 minutes.
Drain beans and place in a shallow serving dish.
Pour onion mixture over beans.
Add salt to taste.

* This can be made a day ahead as follows:
Cover and refrigerate beans and onion mixture separately.
Reheat by boiling beans in water for 2 to 3 minutes and reheating onion mixture in small pan or microwave.

More Across Colorado

DON'T FENCE ME IN

Large-scale cattle ranching on these high plains began during the 1870s. By then, the Plains Indians had been forcibly removed to reservations, and the great buffalo herds had been hunted to near extinction. Here, in southeastern Colorado, the vast grasslands attracted eastern and European capitalists who saw a beef bonanza equal to any gold discovery. And so began the day of the cattleman--a time when the range was open and grass was king. To help the great cattle barons, Colorado required would-be sodbusters to fence roaming cattle *out* of their property. The open range prevailed until the late 1890s, when a network of rails, windmills, and barbed wire opened this region to farmers.

More Across Colorado

Green Beans Supreme

This dish may be refrigerated and then baked. *

½ cup sliced onion
1 tablespoon minced parsley
2 tablespoons butter
1 tablespoon flour
1 teaspoon salt
¼ teaspoon pepper
½ teaspoon lemon zest
1 cup sour cream
5 cups cooked green beans
½ cup grated cheddar cheese
2 tablespoons melted butter
½ cup dry bread crumbs

Cooking time: 20 minutes
Serves: 6 to 8

Cook onion and parsley in the butter.
Add flour, salt, pepper and lemon zest.
Stir until well blended.
Stir in sour cream.
Add beans and heat through.
Turn into a 10x6x1½-inch baking dish.
Top with the grated cheese.
Combine melted butter and bread crumbs.
Sprinkle on top.
Broil on low setting until heated through.

* Dish may be refrigerated, then baked at 450° until heated through.

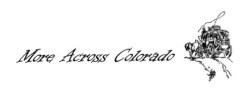

More Across Colorado

Tepees

TRAIL UNDER SIEGE

Kiowa and Comanche Indians migrated to these prairies in the 1700s, followed by Cheyennes and Arapahos in the early 1800s. The region's infinite grasslands, thick bison herds, and brisk fur trade made for prosperous, if not entirely harmonious, living; the allied Cheyennes and Arapahos warred frequently against the Comanches and Kiowas (who gradually moved south) until 1840, when the tribes agreed to a historic peace. In 1851 the United States granted most of eastern Colorado to the Cheyennes and Arapahos, but when gold rushers began stampeding through after 1859, strife erupted anew, this time between whites and Indians. One tragic episode (the 1864 Hungate Massacre) occurred about fourteen miles northwest of Kiowa. Though they fought for their homeland, the Indians were badly outgunned and outnumbered; by 1869 they had been banished from Colorado's plains forever.

Denver-bound travelers could save distance and time on the Smoky Hill Trail, but only if willing to risk death by Indian attack. The trail bisected the Cheyennes' and Arapahos' homeland, and the tribes kept it under siege almost continuously in the late 1860s. One branch earned notoriety as the Starvation Trail after an 1859 Gold Rush party met a disastrous end, but the Smoky Hill became a main highway to Denver in 1865, when the Butterfield Overland Dispatch began running stagecoaches on it. With fortified stage stops every few miles the route was reasonably well defended, but passengers never rested easy, as the war whoop might go up at any moment. Enough people took their chances, though, to keep the Smoky Hill Trail busy until the 1870 opening of the Kansas Pacific Railroad.

More Across Colorado

Holiday Asparagus

1 oven bag, regular size (10x16 inches)
1 tablespoon flour
¼ cup water
2 cloves garlic, minced
2 pounds asparagus spears
1 medium-size red bell pepper, cut into strips
8 large fresh mushrooms, sliced
2 tablespoons butter

Cooking time: 9 to 11 minutes
Serves: 8 to 10

Shake flour in oven bag; place in 13x9x2-inch microwave-safe baking dish.
Add water and garlic to oven bag.
Squeeze oven bag to blend ingredients.
Add asparagus, red pepper and mushrooms.
Arrange ingredients in an even layer in oven bag.
Dot with butter.
Close oven bag with nylon tie; cut six ½-inch slits in top.
Microwave on high for 9 to 11 minutes, or until asparagus is tender.
To serve, remove from oven bag and transfer vegetables to serving dish.
Spoon sauce from baking bag over the vegetables.

More Across Colorado

LA VETA

Col. John Francisco was no town builder. After purchasing a 48,000-acre chunk of a Mexican land grant in 1858, this veteran of the Santa Fe trade raised an adobe homestead, leased the rest of his holdings to ranchers and farmers, and sat on his porch with cronies from the frontier days. But when the Denver & Rio Grande came through in 1876, a town inevitably followed. Settlers flocked in as the tracks pushed up 9,900-foot La Veta Pass, then the world's highest rail crossing, and by the next year fledgling La Veta had about 400 denizens. After a brief commercial heyday, the community returned to the easy agrarian lifestyle that Colonel Francisco loved so well. He died in 1902, but his genial pulse is still felt in La Veta.

Col. John Francisco

More Across Colorado

Mexican Corn Pie

*This recipe may be baked and refrigerated for up to 3 days before serving. ***

3 large eggs, beaten
8.5-ounce can cream-style corn
10-ounce package frozen corn, thawed and
    drained
4-ounce can diced green chiles, optional
½ cup butter, melted
½ cup yellow cornmeal
1 cup sour cream
4 ounces cheddar cheese cut in ½-inch cubes
4 ounces Monterey Jack cheese, cut in ½-inch
    cubes
½ teaspoon salt
1¼ teaspoons Worcestershire sauce, optional

Cooking time: 1 hour to 1½ hours
Serves: 6

Grease a 10-inch pie plate generously with shortening or oil cooking spray
In a large bowl, combine all ingredients.
Pour into pie plate and bake uncovered at 350° for 1 hour to 1½ hours.
Test at the end of 1 hour by inserting knife in center.

* Pie may be baked and refrigerated for up to 3 days.
When ready to use, reheat pie at 350° for about 20 minutes.

Note: This may be used as a main dish or side dish.

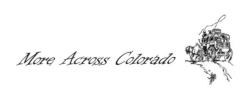

More Across Colorado

PALMER'S CITY

William Jackson Palmer established Colorado Springs in 1871 as a resort for "people of means and social standing." His intentions were twofold: To appease his wife, Queen Mellen, a New York socialite who found the West badly lacking in refinement; and to attract investment capital for his expanding rail network. The settlement succeeded on both counts. With its scenic wonders, healthy climate, and opulent hotels, Colorado Springs grew popular with authors, painters, and persons of high social standing. It gained particular favor among the English, who settled in such great numbers the town was dubbed Little London. Though it owed its existence to Palmer's Denver & Rio Grande, Colorado Springs wasn't just another railroad town; it represented the crown jewel of a vast rail empire.

General William Jackson Palmer

More Across Colorado

Mexican Spoon Bread

1 cup cornmeal
1 teaspoon salt
½ teaspoon baking soda
¾ cup milk
⅓ cup coking oil
2 eggs, beaten
14¾-ounce can cream-style corn
4-ounce can diced green chiles, drained
1½ cups shredded sharp cheddar cheese, *or*
      Monterey Jack, *or* half of each

Cooking time: 45 minutes

Combine cornmeal, salt and soda.
Mix well.
Stir in milk and oil, and mix.
Add eggs and corn and blend well.
Spoon half the mixture into a 2-quart greased baking dish
Sprinkle half the chiles on top, then half the cheese.
Repeat layers, ending with the cheese.
Bake, uncovered, in preheated oven at 350° for about 45 minutes or until wooden pick inserted in center comes out clean.
To serve, spoon from casserole onto serving plate.

Note: This can be served as a vegetable with any kind of meat or poultry. By the way, it's eaten with a fork.

Parmesan Potatoes

½ cup butter
¼ teaspoon garlic powder
2 tablespoons Parmesan cheese
5 medium potatoes

Cooking time: 1 hour
Serves: 5

Melt butter in a 9x13-inch pan.
Stir in the garlic powder and Parmesan cheese.
Scrub potatoes and cut in half lengthwise.
Roll in butter and place cut-side down in pan.
Bake at 325° for 1 hour.

More Across Colorado

The Broadmoor Hotel opened in 1918. The hotel's architects also designed Grand Central Station, and the Ritz-Carlton, Vanderbilt, and Belmont hotels in New York City.

More Across Colorado

PALMER'S CITY II

The Cripple Creek gold strike of 1890 changed Colorado Springs forever. Without warning, Palmer's exclusive colony was overrun by men of crass ambition, their sweating animals and dusty boots soiling the genteel avenues to town. Little London became less retiring and more enterprising, more like a typical frontier community; by 1900, Tejon Street was lined with mining concerns and the local population had tripled. As mining fever waned in the early twentieth century, tourism and tuberculosis sanatoriums kept Colorado Springs on the map. Fifty years later, another boom reshaped Colorado Springs: Fort Carson, the U.S. Air Force Academy, and the North American Air Defense Command (NORAD), all installed during and after World War II, made this a military hub. With the influx of jobs and federal money, Colorado Springs boomed anew, becoming one of the great cities of the Rockies.

Roasted Red Potatoes

1 pound small red potatoes
1 tablespoon olive oil
½ teaspoon salt
⅛ teaspoon pepper
2 tablespoons freshly grated Parmesan cheese

Cooking time: 40 minutes
Serves: 4

Cut potatoes into ¼-inch slices. Place in sealable plastic bag.
Add olive oil, salt and pepper to potatoes.
Seal the bag and shake well to mix.
Place potatoes in a greased 9x13-inch baking dish.
Spread out potatoes to a single layer; sprinkle with Parmesan.
Cover tightly with aluminum foil.
Bake at 350° for 40 minutes or until tender.

Southern Sweet Potatoes

3 cups canned sweet potatoes
1 cup sugar
2 eggs, beaten
½ teaspoon salt
½ cup *each* milk and melted butter
1½ teaspoons vanilla

Topping:
½ cup brown sugar
⅓ cup each flour and melted butter
1 cup chopped pecans

Cooking time: 30 minutes
Serves: 8

Combine all ingredients except for topping, and spoon into a 9-inch-square shallow baking dish.

Topping:
Combine topping ingredients and sprinkle on top of sweet potato mixture.
Bake at 325° for 30 minutes.

More Across Colorado

Hispano families like this one, c. 1890, were among the many settlers who helped to populate and develop Trinidad and Las Animas County.

HISPANO COLORADO

In 1620, when English colonists landed in the New World and stepped on Plymouth Rock, Spain had already established an eighty-year occupation in the present American Southwest; not until 1848 did Mexico cede to the United States these lands south of the Arkansas River. Today, Hispano influence in the state can be seen not only in the faces of its people but also in the names on the face of the land. Trinidad is Spanish for Trinity, while the Purgatoire River was originally named *Rio de las Animas Perdidas en Purgatorio*, or River of Lost Souls in Purgatory. The Sangre de Cristo (Blood of Christ) Mountains rise to the west, as do the twin Spanish Peaks. In architecture, in the arts, in food, in language, and in a thousand ways Colorado (Spanish for red) proudly reflects Hispano tradition and culture.

Tater Tot Casserole

This recipe can be prepared the day before. *

10½-ounce can cream of mushroom soup
12-ounce can evaporated milk
4-ounce can of mushrooms, drained
4-ounce can green chiles, optional
1½ cups grated cheddar cheese
32-ounce bag frozen Tater Tots
1 large onion, chopped

Cooking time: 1 hour
Serves: 12 to 14

Whisk soup and milk until well blended. Fold in remaining ingredients, except cheese. Pour into greased 2-quart baking dish.
* *Let stand for 1 hour or overnight in refrigerator.*

Bake at 350° for 1 hour, until bubbly.
Top with cheddar cheese before the last 15 minutes.

Story: Our favorite way to entertain as a Marine Corps family was to have friends and neighbors over for a Sunday brunch. Now, since we have come home to Trinidad, Colorado, this recipe is a family favorite as well. *JoAnn Simpleman*

Yummy Carrots

4 cups grated carrots
½ cup apple juice, *or* apple cranberry juice
½ cup Craisins

Cooking time: 45 minutes
Serves: 8

Combine in casserole dish and cover.
Bake at 350° degrees for 30 to 45 minutes.

More Across Colorado

TRINIDAD

Trinidad, c. 1879.

Rising on the Santa Fe Trail in 1860, Trinidad quickly emerged as a farming, ranching, and freighting mecca, and nearby coal seams spawned a mining boom in the late 1800s. By then Trinidad lay at the heart of a thriving commercial network, with major arteries heading in all directions. The handsome downtown district - *El Corazón de Trinidad* - reflected the wealth of enterprises headquartered here. Trinidad came to resemble an eastern metropolis in miniature, with three daily newspapers, an opera house, impressive public buildings, and elegant residential neighborhoods. Although the twentieth century brought less spectacular growth, Trinidad remains a vital regional center, its grand old buildings still radiating power and prestige.

More Across Colorado

Vegetables in Wine Sauce

1 pound small boiling onions, peeled
3 cups 1-inch carrot pieces
4 cups water
1 teaspoon salt
4 cups 1-inch celery pieces
¾ cup butter
½ cup flour
½ teaspoon dry mustard
¾ teaspoon salt
⅛ teaspoon pepper
2 cups half-and-half
⅔ cup dry white wine
¼ cup grated Parmesan cheese
paprika, optional
parsley, optional

Cooking time: 45 minutes
Serves: 8 to 10

Combine onions, carrots, water and salt in large saucepan.
Bring to boil.
Cover pan and reduce heat; simmer for 10 minutes.
Add celery, return to full boil.
Cover pan and reduce heat; simmer for 10 minutes.
Remove from heat and drain. Set aside.
Melt butter in heavy saucepan over low heat.
Add flour, mustard, salt and pepper. Stir until smooth.
Cook 1 minute, stirring constantly.
Gradually add the cream.
Cook over medium heat, stirring constantly, until mixture is very thick.
Gradually stir in the wine.
Remove from heat.
Pour cream-wine mixture over reserved vegetables. Stir to combine.
Pour into a lightly greased, 2-quart, shallow baking dish.
Sprinkle with the Parmesan cheese, as well as paprika and/or parsley for added color, if desired.
Bake at 350° for 20 minutes or until bubbly.

More Across Colorado

George Bent and his Cheyenne wife, Magpie, 1867.

FORT LARAMIE TREATY

The Fort Laramie Treaty of 1851 promised the Cheyennes and Arapahos that the territory between the Arkansas and Platte rivers would be theirs forever. Forever lasted ten years. The 1859 Pikes Peak gold rush brought thousands of immigrants into Indian land; two years later a new treaty restricted the tribes to a small, remote reservation in south-central Colorado, far from gold country. Big Sandy Creek - Sand Creek to history - flows just west of today's US 40 and marked the reserve's eastern boundary. But many Westerners objected to any Indian presence. On November 29, 1864, sixty miles downstream from Hugo, U.S. troops wantonly attacked Cheyenne Chief Black Kettle's peaceful village, killing several hundred men, women, and children. The infamous Sand Creek Massacre opened years of High Plains conflict that ended only with the tribes' forced removal to lands in Oklahoma, Wyoming, and Montana.

More Across Colorado

Zucchini Casserole

2 packages crescent rolls (16)
½ cup grated Parmesan cheese
3 to 4 medium-size zucchini, halved lengthwise
      and sliced ¼-inch thick
3 cups sliced fresh mushrooms
1 large onion, chopped
salt
pepper
garlic salt
16 ounces sour cream
¼ cup flour
1 cup Monterey Jack shredded cheese

Cooking time: 40 to 55 minutes
Serves: 12

Lightly grease a 9x13-inch pan.
Unroll 1 package of rolls; press evenly in pan and seal perforations.
Sprinkle with ¼ cup of the Parmesan cheese.
Bake at 350° for 10 to 15 minutes or until golden.
Place zucchini, mushrooms, onion, salt, pepper and garlic salt (to taste) in steamer or microwave.
Cook until crisp-tender.
Stir together sour cream and flour.
Stir in vegetables, and pour over crust.
Top with Monterey Jack cheese.
Unroll second package of crescent rolls and place on top of cheese.
Sprinkle with remaining ¼ cup of Parmesan cheese.
Bake at 350° for 30 to 40 minutes.

More Across Colorado

Hay harvest, southeastern Colorado.

MAKING THE DESERT BLOOM

Colorado's southeastern plains - a spectacular short-grass country of rolling hills, broad river valleys, and rugged canyons - excited comments from early Spanish and American explorers. In 1601, Don Juan de Oñate wrote of "extensive and delightful plains." In 1706, Juan de Ulibarri marveled at the "great fertility of the land." One hundred years later, two American explorers - Lt. Zebulon M. Pike in 1806, and Maj. Stephen H. Long in 1820 - saw only a "desert." Yet, this wasteland was rich enough to support untold numbers of buffalo, antelope, and deer. Later, it would accommodate great herds of cattle, and the sodbuster's plough would bring forth vast crops of wheat, corn, sorghum, and potatoes. Truly, the desert could be made to bloom.

More Across Colorado

Zucchini Fritters

¾ cup ricotta
½ cup chopped scallions
2 tablespoons chopped fresh basil
2 tablespoons chopped, fresh flat-leaf parsley
1 cup all-purpose flour
3 eggs, lightly beaten
3 cups shredded zucchini
½ cup shredded Parmesan cheese
1 teaspoon salt
¼ teaspoon pepper
4 tablespoons olive oil, divided
lemon zest for garnish

Cooking time: 20 to 30 minutes
Yield: 24 to 28

In a large bowl, combine first 4 ingredients.
Stir in flour.
Add eggs; stir well.
Stir in zucchini, Parmesan, salt and pepper.
Heat 2 tablespoons oil in large non-stick skillet over medium heat.
Drop batter by tablespoonfuls into skillet.
Cook 3 to 4 minutes, turning once, until golden.
Remove fritters to baking sheet lined with paper towels and keep warm.
Repeat, using remaining oil as needed.
Arrange on platter and garnish.

More Across Colorado

Recipe Solicitation & Testing Team

Sally Longwell,
  Team Leader
Melanie Eber
Betty Heid
Mary M. (Mimi) Hull
Tanner McCall
Trish McIntyre
Mary Lou Miller
Michelle Simons
Sandra Smith
Shirley Stewart

Consultants to the Team

Chef Anthony
  Polakowski,
  Running Creek
  Farm
Susan Stevens,
  Director, The
  Seasoned Chef
  Cooking School

CHS Regional Museums

Byers-Evans House
  Museum
El Pueblo History
  Museum
Fort Garland Museum
Fort Vasquez Museum
Georgetown Loop
  Historic Mining &
  Railroad Park
Healy House Museum
  & Dexter Cabin
Trinidad History
  Museum
Ute Indian Museum

Testing Volunteers

Janice Alsum
Carol Anderson
Julie Barton
Cindy Beer
Sybil Binder
Gloria Bradfield
Barbara Brancio

Barbara Brown
Joanne Brummel
Shelly Burnett
Tammy Card
Nancy Chamberlin
Susan Chambers
Joi Chavez
Kim Coleman
Denise Cross
Dianne Czeczok
Robin Dary
Fran Davidson
Carol Dietz
Melanie Eber
Mary McInnes
  Flowers
Annette Fricke
Jennifer Fugita
Charlene Gail
Marianne Galbreath
Nancy Gapter
Diana Gilmore
Brenda Goodwin
Carla Goodwin
Mary Ellen Green
Margaret Greivel
Christine Harkness

Betty Heid
Louise Hickman
Eleanor Hixon
Julie Holmes
Mary M. (Mimi) Hull
Maggie Jamsay
Sharon Jarrett
Susan Johnson
June Korte
Linda Kyle
Diana Longwell
Sally Longwell
Sheila Longwell
Tanner McCall
Trish McIntyre
Mary Lou Miller
Margaret Mills
Dee Morrison
Shirley Moschetti
Mindee Myers
Debbie Philps
Valerie Powell
Rudy Prinz
Becca Reidy
Dianne Rodgers
Polly Rodriguez
Jim Rose

Mary Nelle Ryan
Tonya Schlener
Judy Schroedl
Michelle Simons
Bob Smith
Denise Smith
Jerry Smith
Sandra Smith
Bev Stahl
Edna Stewart
Shirley Stewart
Susan Stone
Karen Suppes
Paula Swanson
Deidre Warner
Chris Watson
Julie Whitcomb
Paulette Whitcomb
Lola Williams
Rita Workman
Isabel Zimmerman

More Across Colorado

Recipe Contributors

Victoria Alcorta
Carole Anderson
Luann Anderson
Barb Arnett
Sam'l P. Arnold
  The Fort,
  Morrison
J. P. (Judy) Atwater
LouRae (Cookie)
  Baker
Bette Beers
Alison Blackburn
Diane Boyd
Em Broughton
Barbara Bushacher
Anne Button
Angela Caudill
Lorraine Chesley
Marjorie Coate
Denise Cross
Dianne Czeczok
Mike Dafini
Nancy Dafini
Janice Dean
Mary Jean DiLisio
Connie Dineen

Carol Mitchell Duncan
Melanie Eber
James Finnerty
  Director,
  Governor's
  Residence
Mary McInnes Flowers
Annette Fricke
Charlene Gail
Marianne Galbreath
Elaine Garrison
Chris Geddes
Ginny Gelbach
Miriam Graetzer
  Quilt House Bed &
  Breakfast, Estes Park
Margaret Greivel
Mary Hartley
Mary Hartman
Betty Heid
Eleanor Hixon
Margaret Hodd
Truett Hollis
Audrey Holmes
Mary M. (Mimi) Hull
Maggie Jamsay
Dottie Jeltema

Linda Jensen
Joanne Johnson
Susan Johnson
Marian Jump
Irene Kell
Marcia Koester
June Korte
Linda Kyle
Lillian LaFleur
Sally Longwell
Karen Mandel
Gertrude Spencer Marr
Charles D. Martin
Pat McDonnell
Leo McGinnis
Libbie McIntyre
Trish McIntyre
Jean Omohundro
  McLaughlin
Mary Lou Miller
Sarah Miller
Margaret Mills
Jane Modica
Winifred Modica
Margaret Moyer
Mindee Myers
Donna Nading

Wendy Nading
Pat Nading-Amman
Frances Owens
  Colorado's
  First Lady
Flo Pancir
Nancy Parma
Lucille Lotito Pesce
Fern Pierce
Bill Price
Dennis Price
Arlene Rehbein
Shawn Reynolds
Gloria Rosener
Gwenn Rosener
Vicky Rosener
Lois Ryan
Lorraine Salazar
Maureen Scanlon
Jean Schrader
Marie Shaw
Sidney Sheldon
Michelle L. Simons
JoAnn Simpleman
Jill Skorpen

Sandra Smith
Katheryn Staples
Shirley Stewart
Linda Stransky
Phyllis Stransky
Virginia Sugg
Judith Sullivan
Carol Toth
  Manager,
  Highland's Garden
  Café, Denver
Marj VanWyk
Clair E. Villano
Diedre Warner
Shanna Weatherford
Vicki Whelan
Paulette Whitcomb
Carol Williams
Jeanne Williams
Rita Workman
Gloria Zakus

More Across Colorado

More Across Colorado

More Across Colorado

More Across Colorado

RECIPE INDEX, BY CATEGORY

Some entries within a category are slightly out of alphabetical order because of space exigencies.

More Across Colorado

More Across Colorado